The Travels and Tribulations of an About 6'10" Basketball Globetrotter

By Kevin Owens

Foreword by
NBA Veteran Chucky Brown

"Kevin Owens has lived a basketball life less ordinary. We often hear about professional players who are selected and celebrated early on, and who sail through the glitzy prep circuit and make it to the highest levels of the game. But as Owens' terrific book reminds us, some players have to grind and endure to make their dreams come true. And often their stories are the most entertaining."

-Lang Whitaker currently works for the Memphis Grizzlies as the General Manager of Grizz Gaming, and as a contributor to Grind City Media. Additionally, Lang works as a contributor to GQ Magazine.

"American basketball fans 'know' about guys 'playing overseas' because it's such a common occurrence. Their favorite high school or college player can't quite stick in the NBA but isn't ready to hang up his kicks so he goes overseas. But what the hell happens over there? Given the complete dearth of coverage in American media about basketball in foreign countries, smart fans are hungry to learn what it's like. In Overseas Famous, long-time pro baller Kevin Owens teaches us, sharing the good, bad and the ugly of overseas basketball. Bonus points for a very cool foreword from the great Chucky Brown, too."

-Ben Osborne is Senior Features Editor for Fox Sports Digital. He was previously Editor-in-Chief of Bleacher Report and SLAM (where he first got familiar with Kevin via his recurring blog posts from overseas)

Edited by Dr. Cheryl Robinson

Published by Overseas Famous LLC

Visit our website at **overseasfamous.com**

Book Cover designed and photographed by the great Karen McCandless of Karen McCandless Photography

Contact author: **overseasfamous@gmail.com**

Instagram: **@Knockout2515**

Twitter: **@Overseasfamous**

ISBN: 978-1-7372822-0-4

To Livy,

I wrote this book for you. I wanted you to realize that I am not just a regular dad; I'm a cool dad. I want you to always know that you make me so proud every day. I love you very much. Always remember life will be hard. There will be both good times and bad. Learn from these triumphs and tribulations and always keep improving. The crown is waiting for you.

Love, Dad

Foreword

Having played in the NBA for thirteen years, won an NBA Championship, coached in the G-League, and been a scout, I have experienced many different types of players. Kevin is one of the memorable ones. Not only was he a great player, but he was personable. He became more than just a player I coached; he became a friend.

When I first met Kevin, it was during my first year as an assistant coach in the G-League. What sticks out most was how nice of a person Kevin was. That is until you pissed him off. He was always a good rebounder. I can remember many games where Kevin had a double-double, getting double-digit points and rebounds. But he was just so nice to people out on the court. Coach Davidson used to do things or say things to get Kevin mad. I remember a particular night we were playing in Mobile, Alabama. The team had a guy that was supposedly the best rebounder in the league. I remember Kevin having sixteen or seventeen rebounds against them that game. That was probably the angriest I had seen him play. He used to always like to shoot with his left hand around the basket. Coach Davidson was always cool with it until he missed one. Kevin will always be one of my favorite players just simply because he had a great attitude and always approached the game the right way.

I saw the improvement in Kevin's game from the first day together until he decided to go overseas and extend his career. As a coach, it makes me feel good to see him doing well and staying active around the game that I know he loves. It also feels good whenever he asks me for advice.

Everyone knows me from my time playing in the NBA. However, I did spend some time playing basketball overseas. The funny thing is that every player who has played international basketball has similar stories with the peculiarities of the experiences.

I played overseas in Italy for a very short time. The situation was not a good one, but I loved the city. Florence was amazing; the owners of the team not so much. They once tried to charge me a $30,000 fine because I walked by the owner and didn't say hello. They had a hard time understanding that I didn't speak Italian and the coach didn't speak English. I actually never unpacked my bags. They moved me from one hotel to another over the course of three months. After they finally gave me a house, I had had enough and bought a ticket home.

Very few people talk about these types of experiences. Kevin's book will help up-and-coming basketball players be prepared for what lies ahead in their careers. I wish I had someone or a book to help me navigate the craziness of overseas basketball.

Chucky Brown

13 years in the NBA; 12 different teams
NBA Championship with the Houston Rockets
CBA Championship with the Yakima Sunkings
Coached 8 years in the NBA Development League
Scouted 7 years for the New Orleans Pelicans

Table of Contents

Part Three

Overseas Nonsense

"Let us not waste our time in idle discourse! Let us do something, while we have the chance!" (Samuel Beckett, Waiting for Godot)

Prologue

The loud bass resonating from Room 218 shook the light fixtures illuminating the hallway of the Richmond, Virginia Hampton Inn. I stood at the door, staring at the paper sleeve which held the plastic magnetic key, trying to figure out why the beautiful receptionist had given me a key to what was, apparently, a wild hotel party. *Maybe she wants me?* I thought, before my lack of confidence took over and ruined whatever excitement had crept into my mind. I looked down at the paper again. Room 218 was scribbled on the top. I looked back at the door, which danced to the beat of the muffled song I could not yet make out—room 2-1-8. My Monmouth University duffle bag containing copious amounts of basketball gear hung at my side, putting a strain on my already weary shoulders. I had just completed my first day as a participant in an overseas basketball exposure camp at Virginia Commonwealth University, and my body needed a rest.

I did not check into the room earlier that day, instead opting to stay at the gym where there was more of a chance for all the EXPOSURE implied in the brochure my agent had emailed me a few weeks earlier. It was now ten at night, and I, selfishly, had not thought about the random player I would share this hotel room with due to the lack of funds I had at the time. All I knew was that in room 218, there was a comfortable bed waiting for me. But something about the music pulsating through the door frame made me think that rest would have to wait. Grabbing the door's handle, I could feel the vibrations from within the door frame structure. I unsheathed the key and placed it into the slot. The contraption buzzed, the light turned green, and I slowly turned the handle.

The door continued trembling as I slowly opened it. I was greeted by a bass beat so loud it rattled my stomach, creating an almost nauseous feeling. The distinct sound of R. Kelly's romantic words, Feelin On Ya Booty, overpowered the other noises I would soon be exposed to. It was the early 2000's R. Kelly before we realized he was writing those lyrics about high schoolers.

The loud music that shook my soul was attempting to drown out the equally loud moaning of the three girls being pleasured on the two queen-sized beds. I stood there dumbfounded. Not only were there three naked ladies, but several dudes were positioning themselves on the soft, comfortable bed I assumed I'd be sleeping on that night. *Oh Shit!*, I thought as I froze, not able to look away from the hardcore pornography taking place just three feet from me.

"Who the fuck is that?" one of the girls shouted as I stood completely still, hoping her eyesight was based on movement, like a T-Rex. I didn't think this was the time to introduce myself as the roommate and ask how they fared in the games today. I also thought it'd be inappropriate to disrobe and join in.

Instead, I shrugged and yelled, "Whoops," as I quickly exited the room. I stood wide-eyed with my back against the hallway wall as the door clicked shut, trying to figure out what to do next. I was understandably frazzled after witnessing three naked women in an orgy.

Tomorrow will be so weird, I thought, as the realization that I had seen my fellow campers and worse, they had seen me settled into my mind. Hopefully, because of all the sex, they would not recognize me as the perverted guy who walked in on their fun.

And hopefully, their legs would be as tired as my old coach told me would happen after having sex the night before a game. Thinking about it now, he most likely told us that to deter me from having sex, which I didn't need help with, as preventing girls from having sex with me was something that came naturally.

I leaned against the wall and laughed at the circumstances that brought me to this spot. All the hard work and sweat, persistence, injuries and tears that led me to that exact moment. The heartfelt memory montage playing in my head in the hallway of a Hampton Inn was suddenly interrupted when I noticed that something felt different, and it was not what was going on in my pants. The weight that had been residing in my right hand was gone. I smacked the back of my head against the wall in frustration. *My bag! I must have dropped my bag in there.*

I could not wait and go back in later. That would be far too embarrassing, plus my car keys were in the side pocket. I had already breached the door, and the unsaid Guy Code prohibited me from telling the hotel about the wild orgy going on in my room. This situation needed to be resolved immediately, as returning to that room ever again was not going to happen. I knew I had to go back in and grab it. I shook my head, looked to the sky, and closed my eyes. *This is gonna suck*, I said to myself as I reentered the key into the slot. After hearing the familiar buzz, I stepped back into the sex party.

"YOOOOOOO! C'mon man, we're busy here!" the one dude shouted at me.

"I'm so sorry. I'm so sorry," I frantically repeated while grasping at the air, trying to find the whereabouts of my bag and attempting to cover my eyes, as though that would have made the situation any less awkward. I shuffled through the darkness for what felt like an hour but was only a matter of seconds. It just feels like an hour when six angry, naked people are staring at you. I finally reached and grabbed hold of the handle. "Got it," I yelled, looking up in excitement as the others just glared at me. It was that kind of behavior that kept me from receiving orgy invites. The door slammed closed for the last time behind me.

I ran a personal financial diagnostic check. I couldn't afford another hotel room, and it was 10 pm! I still had two more days left. What was I supposed to do? Where was I supposed to shower? Desperate, tired, and broke, I made my way back to the parking lot, and the only option that remained, the Chevy Silverado 2500HD which would double as my shelter for the night.

It was a hot and humid July evening, and the mosquitos were out in full force. I pressed the unlock button on my key fob and opened the door. The heat from a full day under the hot Virginia sun had turned the vehicle into a sweatbox. I knew I could not blast the AC unit all night, or I would run out of gas. I rolled down the windows allowing some relief from the sweltering interior of my truck. I tried to lay in the backseat. It didn't take long before I discovered my 6-foot 10-inch frame was not going to fit. I pulled the latch on the side of the driver and passenger seats and pushed them to the dashboard, hoping that this would give me a little extra room. It just created an odd contortion of my body that, along with lack of sleep, would probably put some hindering on my joints, an essential part of any high-level athlete's body. The only other option was the 8-foot bed that I used to haul junk for my old middle school coach that spring.

The summer heat had not subsided when the moon rose but rather intensified, causing the metal frame of my black truck to retain the heat. I had a thin sheet covering the back seat, used primarily to stop the orange dog hairs from my somewhat asshole of a dog Nelly, from integrating with the cloth seats. I laid the thin sheet down, grabbed some clothes, which would double as pillows, from my bag, and climbed up into the, ironically named bed of my truck. My makeshift sleeping arrangement on a heated metal mattress was just the beginning.

As I reflected on my day, while occasionally shooing away mosquitos, I looked up at the stars. I wondered several things: *Was I going to be murdered in the back of my truck, parked in the darkness, next to a large creepy wooded area? Were the girls each paired with a guy, or was it just the old find-a-hole-approach?* I was so close to my dream of playing professional basketball. The visualization of one day playing on an NBA court helped me relaxed.

I spent the first night of my first professional basketball experience sleeping in the back of my truck while the room I paid for was used as a makeshift brothel. Unbeknownst to me at the time, this incident would become just a tiny blip on the weirdness scale of a long and very strange basketball career, which would take me to all the ends of the earth.

Part 1

Domestic Career

Chapter 1

Humble Beginnings

It was a Saturday morning, not unlike any other March morning in the late 90s. The weather had gone from frigid to simply cold. Honeycomb filled my cereal bowl. My mom had started planning her spring garden, where the perennials were planted to supplement the annuals that still lay dormant underground. But this was not just any Saturday morning; it was the day the All-South Jersey team would be featured in the Courier-Post, Southern New Jersey's newspaper option for local news. The All-South Jersey team was a status builder. Players who held this title, both past and present, were considered the top basketball players in the Southern part of New Jersey, which is regarded as a breeding ground for high-level athletes.

It was personally important. After three years of sporadic playing time, I was poised to be named an All-South Jersey player. I had an impressive high school senior season, losing only a handful of games compared to our twenty-three wins against a powerhouse schedule while averaging a double-double with sixteen points and twelve rebounds per game. While these stats may not sound exorbitant to the layperson, we played a truly team-oriented style at Camden Catholic High School in Cherry Hill, New Jersey. Camden Catholic was and still remains a powerhouse in the state. For years teams schemed against us, trying to stop the plethora of backdoors and screens. Our system was designed by my first true mentor and high school coach, Jim Crawford. He was one of the most successful and respected coaches in the state. He created a culture of winning, which carried on long after graduation. His system ran multiple plays for multiple players, making opponents locking in on one specific defensive matchup nearly impossible, which is why I had just participated in the twenty-fifth consecutive twenty-win season for this historic program.

In my mind, it had a lot to do with me, as I was a cocky young hothead and thought I was always the best player on the floor. However, at that time, I may have been the only one. Multiple years later, two of my teammates, Zahir McGhee and Matt Crawford, after watching one of our old high school games from the perspective of my dad's handheld camera, supplemented by his unique play-by-play, began to agree with me. I don't think they gave me all the credit...in fact, I believe the quote was, "We always thought you sucked, but after watching the tape, realized you didn't suck that much."

Backhanded compliments aside, I was on a mission that Saturday morning. I shuffled down the driveway and grabbed the paper which held all my hopes and dreams. The article, in the grand scheme of things, was not a big deal. I had already signed a four-year scholarship to play basketball at Monmouth University and was proud of my senior season. But above the bleachers of Camden Catholic's student section, situated just under the rafters, was a wall with 1,000 Point Scorers (not Me), Top Rebounders (also not me) and 1st, 2nd and 3rd Team All-South Jersey (could be me). Having my name on this wall was my goal. The paper, which I held by its protective baggie, was my one shot.

This would not be the first time I was in the newspaper. I had graced those same pages over the past three months with multiple pictures and even a feature story. But the prestige of being named to an All-South Jersey team was my goal since freshman year when I first saw the names of the alumni, who held the honor prior, adorning the wall of Thomas Kennedy Gymnasium. I took off the plastic bag keeping the newspaper dry from the elements, wiped down the milk I spilled pouring my Honeycomb, and flipped to the *Varsity Extra* section. There it was three rows of five images, each captioned with a brief description and their season statistics.

I began scanning the top row, which I had hoped contained the badass headshot I had taken earlier in the year after winning Player of the Week honors. I had tried to look tough by furrowing my brow and giving the camera my sexy eyes, despite my unnaturally skinny frame and the fact that most people could wrap their hands around my scrawny biceps. My eyes danced across the top row annnnnnnnnnnd...NOTHING!

I was slightly confused that my long slender face was not featured but wasn't too surprised as South Jersey had twenty-seven Division One scholarship recipients that year. I understood not being in the top five...top ten yes, top five, eh.

My eyes, like a typewriter, reset to the next line and began to scan. I reached the end, and again my name was not listed. *This is impossible,* I thought. I must have misread. I scanned the first two lines again and sat in shock. I slammed my fist on the table, karmically sending a small wave of Honeycomb milk splattering onto the first two rows. I was beyond pissed. *How could this be?! How could the writers not deem me one of the ten best players in the area after, what I thought, was a great senior season?* I was not happy that my name would be with the third tier All-South Jersey Team forever immortalized on the walls of Camden Catholic.

Disappointed, I went on to see where my face was situated on the 3rd Team. Scanning, scanning, scanning annnnnnnnnnnd...nothing. My name, my face, my furrowed brow and pursed lips, my stats, my description...my high school legacy...gone! I cannot remember the exact phrase that passed through my head at that very moment, but I believe it was something like, *Are you mothereffin' poopin' me right now!*

I was not a starter until my senior year of high school as I developed slowly and was more of a late bloomer. My freshman, sophomore, and junior years were spent as a fragile bud. My senior year was a breakout season, playing in both the South Jersey and New Jersey State All-Star Games. I was even nominated to the McDonald's High School All-American Team, which was a roster of the most elite high school players in the nation. At the time, only 500 players were nominated. And just twenty-four played in the game. While I was not one of those participants, I was nominated.

So, let's recap: I was deemed one of the 500 best basketball players in America, but wasn't one of the fifteen best players in like five counties? This is why I understandably still hold a grudge against the worthless South Jersey basketball writers who nearly destroyed my confidence going forward.

My mom, who had found the crumpled-up paper in the trash can, walked outside to our makeshift basketball court to get an emotional update. She knew this hurt. She also knew she was not the best person to talk to about this, as she was my mom and not my coach. This became more apparent as I uninterruptedly continued shooting as my mom asked if I was ok.

"I'm fine," I responded.

"Maybe talk to Mr. Crawford on Monday," she said, after a few minutes of unsuccessful engagement.

My tutelage under Jim Crawford came long before I arrived at Camden Catholic. He was, in fact, my first ever coach when I unsuccessfully attempted to hit a ball placed on a tee in first grade. I have admired and respected him ever since. He had played college basketball at Lasalle University. He had a brief stint in the NBA and overseas professional basketball before becoming a math teacher and high school basketball coach at Camden Catholic.

I walked into Mr. Crawford's classroom early Monday morning to find him reading the daily sports page, his lips pressed firmly together and his eyes sharp as a hawk. "Hey, Coach," I said, walking towards his desk.

He peaked up from his paper with a slight smirk on his otherwise stern face. "This is about the paper, isn't it?"

I looked down at the floor as my eyes welled up, a combination of sadness and embarrassment. "Yes," I responded, holding back tears. "I just don't understand. I know I am not a 1,000-point scorer or rebounder, but I feel like I contributed to this school, to this program, and my name will never be on that wall."

Mr. Crawford nodded and leaned back in his chair, carefully resting both hands behind his head. "Kevin, you are moving on to bigger games now. And in those games, you will not only be representing Camden Catholic, but you will be representing yourself. You have shown what a good basketball player you are in the past four seasons, but the player you are now is half the basketball player you will become. You will be playing in games that other players on that list could only dream about. A piece of paper or a name on a wall won't change that. Your legacy will not be determined by your high school career, but rather where you go from this point on." He leaned forward and he locked in on my tear-filled eyes. "I want you to strive for higher accolades. Know that this will always be your home, but it is not your final destination."

I looked up, trying not to blink, which would have sent the welled-up tears streaming down my face, and smiled. It was reminiscent of one of those touching moments you see in movies.

"Thanks, Coach," I shrieked, barely audible as the words became muffled while passing over the large lump in my throat. Coach Crawford established an unwavering trust in the men that would coach me going forward that day, solidifying within me an underrated athletic character trait, coachability.

Coachable, a phrase usually reserved for shitty players who are not very good...and incredibly fitting in this context. The walls of my home office are adorned with various forms of coach awards I acquired throughout my life. When I was younger, these awards were quite embarrassing, as they were not the MVP types I was chasing. Although I was becoming an exceptional basketball player, being coachable became my moniker. I was recruited to play on an AAU team between my junior and senior years of high school, a massive win as AAU was relatively new at the time and only the best of the best amateur athletes played. AAU is an organization dedicated to promoting young athletes, allowing them to be seen by more programs and enhancing their chances of playing at the next level.

We were playing in a tournament just outside of Philadelphia. Our coach felt that we needed a boost in morale after getting trounced by a team that we shouldn't have lost to that season. He went around the room, giving each player a unique compliment as some sort of motivational tactic. He honed in on what he felt we excelled at. He started at one end of the locker room, giving out the compliments.

"Jeff," he began, "best jumper. Chris, unbelievable scorer. Ernest, great passer." He revealed his initial guttural reaction to each player as he flew through the praise train. I was four players away, and my mind raced about which of my many strengths he would hone in on. *Would it be my rebounding, my jump shot, my shot-blocking ability? Maybe he would tell me how great my footwork was or how I had become a decent scorer. Maybe he would mention how I had the best hair on the team.* I had been growing it out to look more like Brandon Lee in *The Crow* because, at the time, I thought chicks dug the goth, grunge guys who seemed dangerous. My thoughts were interrupted.

"Owens," he said, pointing his finger at me. "You are incredibly…" *Here it comes. What am I the best at, Coach?!* "…coachable," he finished. *Coachable, that's it?! Son of a bitch.* I looked around at the reactions of my teammates, who were equally uncomfortable with this second-rate compliment.

Although I was not remarkably proud of this moment, it did give me a leg up on the competition. Being coachable was a way for me to get noticed by collegiate coaches who, while enamored with my height, frowned upon my weight and coordination. One coach informed me that while my body would fill out and my skills would improve, watching me stare intently into my coach's eyes during the game and follow every direction flawlessly made them pursue me as a potential recruit.

AAU was the start of my collegiate recruitment, a remarkably absurd process, where grownups attempt to impress the underage prospects by calling and sending affectionate notes to sway them to choose their college. The college basketball recruiting process begins and ends with a phone call. In between is a carousel of letters, meetings, visits, promises and decisions.

I was introduced to the college recruiting process during my freshman year of high school when my brother began being wooed by several universities. I tagged along during trips to the various campuses and did freshman things like complain about the long drives, make sarcastic comments and run around the different basketball arenas shooting Dude Perfect shots. My parents would yell at me, then explain to the coaches that Geoff and I were very different.

Just a year and a half later, Coach Crawford informed me about a few phone calls he had received from collegiate coaches, inquiring about *ME*. He brought me into his classroom and asked if I was serious about playing basketball at the next level, to which I replied, "Sure!" As a fifteen-year-old, I listed my bike, boobs and Super Nintendo as my favorite things. Considering basketball did not make the top three, my interest was quasi serious. But since my family was already knee-deep in this process, and my jealousy of my brother's attention was mentally debilitating, I decided to pursue this dream.

Generic letters from multiple NCAA basketball programs began arriving in the mail. Most of these inquiries were sent out to anyone who stood above 6-feet 5-inches and could spell their name correctly. The pile grew as I proved myself a serviceable basketball player who could not only write my name correctly but perform more daunting tasks, like book reports and fractions. Being that I was super awkward in high school with zero game, I used to purposely drop letters on the ground so that the pretty girls became well aware I was going places.

I quickly realized that the ladies weren't impressed by the letters, and I needed to back up my subtle hints by applying myself on the court. I attended multiple camps over the summer, which were labeled invitational, despite anyone with a checkbook and a varsity letter having access. They were The Pocono Invitational Camp in the middle of nowhere; Eastern Invitational on the campus of Rutgers University; and Five Star Invitational in Pittsburgh, who offered me an invite despite being more of a Two Star recruit. The highlights were as follows:

- Getting my first in-game dunk and subsequently running into the pole that held up the basket at the Eastern Invitational Camp, splitting my lip wide open.

- Drinking so much Gatorade that I began vomiting red while running down the court at the Pocono Invitational Camp. The camp nurse initially thought I was puking blood. It turned out to be the overdose on red Gatorade, a novelty for me at the time as it was not something my family ever purchased, and every cooler was filled with this delicious liquid energy at all times.

- Calling my mom from the Five Star Camp overly elated because Christian Laettner, my idol, was a counselor that week and earlier that day told me I had the best footwork he had seen that summer. "Mom, the guy who hit the biggest shot in NCAA Tournament history based mostly on impeccable footwork, told me I had great footwork." Not to my awareness, there was a long line of campers waiting to use the payphone. When I turned around after I hung up, I noticed my peers laughing at me for the over-the-top guy love I had conveyed throughout the conversation.

Aside from calamities and embarrassments, I also managed to play some good basketball, making several All-Star

Teams. Additionally, I grew from the 6-foot 2-inch spaz I started as my sophomore year into the 6-foot 9-inch skinny kid with *great* footwork. Handwritten letters began pouring in, a step up from the generic typed letters I had been receiving. Then began phase two of the recruiting process: the phone calls.

I answered the phone at two o'clock in the afternoon on July 1, 1997—the first day phone calls were allowed. Henry Bibby, the then coach at the University of Southern California, was on the other end. Now a quick recap, I had not started a game. Not even when someone was injured. Not for my grade school team and not for my high school team. But I was being offered an official visit and a scholarship by a former NBA player to attend one of the most famous universities on the planet because of my rapidly developing skills and the most orgasmic word in college basketball: potential.

College coaches love potential the same way people love puppies. Sure, it will shit all over your floor and eat your kitchen cabinets initially, but after that first year or two, the potential of that puppy turning into a life-long companion is worth the stress.

Being an oblivious jackass at the time, I hung up the phone after speaking with Coach Bibby, turned to my mom, and told her California was way too far from home. California, the place where young idealists go to chase their dreams. The place that would be serenaded every Tuesday evening during the opening of the show *The O.C.* and was described by Dr. Dre as:

> *"The wild, wild west*
> *A state that's untouchable like Elliot Ness*
> *The track hits ya eardrum like a slug to ya chest*
> *Pack a vest for your Jimmy in the city of sex"*

I passed on an opportunity to go to California and a life of t-shirts and flip flops and sex cities and acting gigs for any tall cinematic monster roles. Looking back, I should have agreed to the scholarship offer over the phone, moved to California, developed earlier, made the NBA, and been one of those energetic ends of the bench guys that, while not being the star, were considered integral to the team.

Bibby's call was the start of the countless others who would call our wall-mounted non-cordless kitchen telephone over the next three months. My social life consisted of sitting at my kitchen table, talking about basketball to middle-aged men whose careers depended on their signing of promising players like myself.

After narrowing down my selection to schools located only on the eastern seaboard, we moved on to the home visit portion of the process. My mom cleaned our home for days to ensure the various coaches traipsed through, believing that I was raised by a family with its shit together. The coaches pulled up in some sort of rental car, put on their suit jackets and shuffled to the door. They would walk in and scope out the home while my mom took their jackets and offered refreshments. The staff assembled in our small living room sitting on the blue floral couch, an unknown casualty of an alcohol-infused evening of mine a few months prior. The head coach would break the ice with a clap of his hands and some sort of spiel about why I should attend their university and why I would be a fit for their basketball team. They would then hand me a booklet with their gear and sneakers, which I would paw through like a baby distracted by a rattle while the coaches talked to my parents about grownup shit.

Some coaches were eloquent salesmen, while some were more intense, sweating profusely throughout the pitch. Some coaches were charming, while some were very straightforward. Each coach brought their unique style to our living room. During our recruiting process, some big names came through the door. Coaches like Jay Wright, John Beilein, Mike Brey, Tim Capstraw and Fran Dunphy sat on the couch pitching the smaller universities they worked for at the time.

I was given three official visits where I spent a weekend at the prospective university, parent-free, offering me a first-hand look at all the perks of being a college basketball player. I watched the Spike Lee joint *He Got Game* a year after my recruiting process and realized that some cool shit really does go down on recruiting trips if you were good. Threesomes, free jerseys, names being announced over the arena's sound system all were the perks of being a highly recruited player. My trips were nothing like that. Girls ignored me. I walked away with zero gear. And the only time my name was announced was when the staff at the local wing staple, Cluck U, let me know my order was ready. My trips were far more uneventful. Drinking some beers, going to some parties, and watching two teammates fight over a girl, which happened twice, on the same night, with the same girl. College, right?

I took my talents to Monmouth University for several reasons. First and foremost, the coaching staff. College coaches tell kids what they want to hear. As a sixteen or seventeen-year-old kid, you know nothing at all. You have very little life experience, and you are defiant and rarely listen to your parents. Basically, you are an asshole. So, when coaches say things, you believe them. Things like *you will start immediately*, or *we will have a new arena soon*, or *you will be the focal point of their offense*. Relying on your parents to guide you is essential to the decision-making process because, let's face it, making life-changing decisions that will alter your entire future at such a young age is wildly irresponsible.

The thing is, no one ever tells you that the charming coach who described your mother's home decor as *lovely* was going to be the same guy calling you a pussy and making you run unthinkably difficult sprint gauntlets at six o'clock in the morning. All because one of your dipshit teammates skipped class.

Every head coach eventually takes on the role of the bad guy. They push you, sometimes in negative ways, and will recruit over you, not because they are dissatisfied with your performance, or they don't genuinely care about you, but because their job is constantly being challenged. The next-man-up mentality is essential in case of injuries or unexpected poor performance or a player not making the grades. This makes having a solid relationship with your head coach during the four years of college no easy task. You are past the developmental years when adolescents are most influenced, but still young enough to not know anything, but think you know everything.

Think about any college relationship. It probably had some rocky times. Maybe you could not agree on things and split up. Then after leaving your high-paying big-city job, you come home to help a struggling bakery get back on its feet. Only to discover your previous love owns the bakery. You throw on an apron, love ensues, and Hallmark plays it in June, prepping the world for Christmas. It is not the other person in the relationship but more the immaturity of the participants.

My collegiate career was an incredible journey, which can be summed up by saying I achieved the three S's of collegiate athletics: I Studied, I Scored and I *Scored*. Meaning, I graduated with a high GPA and enough tutelage and confidence from my Journalism Professor, John Morano, to write a book. I also scored in the bedroom (winky face emoji, kissy face emoji), but I will also gloss over those quickly, as that is how most of those interactions went (sad face emoji). I also scored a lot on the basketball court, scoring over 1,000 points and participating in the NCAA Tournament. This was a dream ever since I cheered on Seton Hall during the dominant Terry Dehere era of the early '90s and emulated him shooting threes on my Nerf Mini Hoop. I remember thinking how cool it would be to play in the Tournament in front of millions of people. In 2001, I was living out my dream.

The 2001 Northeast Conference Championship and a subsequent automatic bid into the NCAA Tournament was a culmination of a quest, which began when I was introduced to Europe in a foreshadowing of what my post-collegiate future would resemble, during the summer of 2000 in Lyon, France.

At that time, the Monmouth University Hawks were going through what some might call a rough patch. We were a proverbial walking-mat for the NEC (Northeast Conference or as my dickhead friends labeled it, Nobody Even Cares). During the two seasons before my arrival on campus, we were 4-23 and 5-21. We finished my freshman year with a record of 12-16, which was respectable for the program at the time. While our records were fairly shitty, we were developing the nucleus that ultimately took us to the first NCAA tournament appearance of my career.

This group flew across the Atlantic together the following summer to tour both France and Switzerland. This was my first trip out of the country, and I had nervous anticipation. I was leaving my comfort zone. After refusing to visit California for fear of being too far away, I was taking a trip to an entirely different continent, with people speaking a foreign language, foods that were new and people that smelled weird. My mom had always told me to take chances and always dance like the symbolism in the Lee Ann Womack song, which is ironic because my body's natural rhythm told me to do the exact opposite. I reluctantly overcame my rampant homesickness and crossed the Atlantic with my teammates.

The foreign tours were a relatively new concept at the time in collegiate athletics. Schools every four years were able to take a summer trip with their team outside the country. The Universities won because it was great exposure for potential international students. The coaches won because it allowed the team to practice and play games during a usual dead period where teams were restricted from having organized basketball activities. And most importantly, the players won as most of us were under twenty-one and could go to bars, get blindly drunk, kiss random French girls, visit famous structures, look at famous paintings, stand on famous streets and stare at topless women on the beaches of Nice, France.

On the court, we were still adjusting to each other. We had not figured out how to become a cohesive unit. We were a young team and had only spent a season learning our place and various roles...and that is when it happened.

It was the fourth quarter of a rough and meaningless game between the Hawks of Monmouth and some random French professional team. We were playing in what felt like a grade school gym in the middle of August. The conditions were steamy, and so were the tempers.

Gerry Crosby, our leader and hard-nosed shooter from Ohio, had the ball on the sideline when a large smelly Frenchmen, who outweighed me by a hundred pounds and hygienically, on the smelliness scale, lied somewhere between musky and homeless, elbowed Gerry directly in the mouth. G retaliated by punching him in the jaw, and the benches cleared. Now I never thought I would be in a brawl. If I did, I guess I envisioned a lot more snapping and dancing. However, this was nothing like what pop culture had taught me in the '80s. It all happened so fast. I remember having an attempted roundhouse kick flung in my direction by a small, unassuming guard who I would never have imagined could perform a spinning roundhouse. I also remember pushing a guy half my size who had his back turned to me, as fighting was not one of my fortes at the time. The next thing I knew, we were being dragged off the court by our coaches. In the locker room after that game, something changed. We developed trust. We were all in this together. If they mess with one of us, they mess with all of us.

We took that attitude into the following season and finished with 21 wins, the most regular season wins in school history. We rolled through the playoffs until the championship game. That night we played St. Francis (NY), with an NCAA tournament bid on the line. You might have watched it on ESPN. It was the game with no fans. We played in front of a raucous crowd of about 200 people. A powerful snowstorm blanketed the east coast, making travel conditions a little shaky. Or at least that was the excuse my roommates gave me.

As the game wound down, we found ourselves in a deep hole. Down by over twenty points with less than fourteen minutes remaining, we started to mount what has now been known in Monmouth inner circles as The Comeback.

Little by little, the lead was chipped away until it was 61-59. That is when our two leaders took over. Rahsaan Johnson, our point guard and one of the best players in school history, drove into the middle of the lane and kicked to Gerry, who buried a three putting us up by one, and we never looked back.

In the NCAA Tournament, we drew quite possibly the best Duke team in school history. Shane Battier, Mike Dunleavy, Jay Williams, Chris Duhon and Carlos Boozer filled out their starting five, making them a tough draw for anyone, let alone one whose starting five weighed a combined 600-pounds. Coach Ron Krayl, our eldest and most experienced coach, wore many hats. He was a defensive specialist, high school gym teacher, and father to teammate Jay Krayl. Coach Krayl stood at mid-court breaking down the Duke roster, in a way you can imagine breaking down a scouting report consisting of two First Team All Americans and six future NBA players, would be. Especially when the man tasked with anchoring our matchup zone defense, yours truly, resembled Slenderman.

"Starting at guard will be Jason Williams," he yelled. "Try to force him to his left, as he is less explosive attacking the basket with his left hand. But don't think he won't put you on a poster if he drives that way."

Good start, I thought as he subsequently went on delivering scouting reports of Shane Battier, Chris Duhon, Carlos Boozer and Mike Dunleavy, each riddled with the perils of their capabilities on the basketball court. We all listened enthusiastically, hoping we could be the first sixteenth seed to take down a giant while I swallowed the fear that sat in the pit of my stomach that we would be destroyed on national television.

Later that day, our starting five sat on a large stage answering questions from the national media. Questions like, "Are you guys excited to be here?" as if we were a charity case who won a trip to Disney World.

Gerry tilted his head and responded, "We didn't come here to get run over. We came to play! We're going to go out there and give it our best shot."

Another reporter who had honed in on my height, and was looking for a sound bite, asked us, a team who plays only a matchup zone, who was guarding Shane Battier? We looked around at each other confused before all eyes locked in on me. I slowly raised my arm.

"I guess that would be me," I answered while the crowd had a good chuckle at my expense. I guess they thought I was joking about the responsibilities of guarding, or in this case, matching up with the NCAA Player of the Year. But I was ready to give him my best shot.

The morning of the game I awoke from a bad dream. I was trying to help my childhood dog who was sniffing around the edge of a steep cliff. I did not want to make any sudden movements, as Pepper was prone to running away. I crept up very slowly, and as I reached for her collar, she darted off the cliff. I jumped to stop her, but it was too late. As I laid with my outstretched arms dangling off the cliff, heartbroken, my body slowly began sliding towards the edge. I was paralyzed and could not stop this momentum. I tried to reach for help, but there was nothing to grab onto. I began plummeting towards the distant ground. Maybe it was the apprehension of the impending game or the near-death experience as our plane nearly fell out of the sky on our flight to North Carolina, but I was not waking up. I could see the ground getting closer and closer. I closed my eyes, lowered my shoulder, and BOOM! I sprung up from my sleeping position like the McAllisters after they overslept in *Home Alone*. I did an appraisal of my surroundings and, while grateful I was in a hotel bed and not dead, I was shaken.

This anxiety became far more intense after my third cup of coffee. I was rarely exposed to caffeine growing up as the caffeine-free Pepsi we bought by the caseload was there to give just a jolt of sugar and carbonation while not stopping my parents from getting a solid night of sleep. This was the game day of all game days. I would be seen on national television that day and had to make sure my body was as energized as possible. *I think I've made a big mistake*, I thought as I walked down the grand stairway of the hotel while trying to stop my hands from shaking uncontrollably as I headed to the bus.

Unbeknownst to us at the time, our pep band and
cheerleaders had taken over the hotel's lobby playing our fight
song as loud as they could as we made our way to our bus. This
was not just a thrill for us but an unexpected thrill to the rest of
the hotel patrons, who probably didn't realize this repetitive noise
would be echoing throughout the building when they booked the
room. This noise pollution added to the growing pressure and
excitement I was already feeling. All these stimuli culminated on
the bus ride over. My hands were shaking, my knees were
shaking, and my mind was a jumbled mess. I needed to calm
down, but how? I had never been in a situation like this before.
All the pre-tournament pomp and circumstance was fun and
exciting, but now it was time to perform. I was two seconds away
from a full-on panic attack when my teammate Jay Dooley walked
by me.

"O-Dog," he said, which was my nickname at the time,
"last night, I did some crazy shit to that girl. I'm pretty sure she's
coming. I'll point her out to you."

I laughed nervously and looked at Dools (his nickname at
the time), who was so relaxed. It was calming. I had concentrated
strictly on the game and not remotely about just being a kid and
enjoying this experience. This was the greatest basketball moment
of my life thus far, and I was wasting it worrying about what
could go wrong. I took a deep breath and smiled. I was not going
to waste another minute being scared. Not now, not ever. My
hands slowly relaxed as I took the floor to the sold-out arena.

It was a surreal experience. I had played in packed high
school gymnasiums exceeding fire code occupancy, and
occasionally Boylan Gym at Monmouth University would be
packed, but nothing compared to Greensboro Coliseum. The
occupancy for the arena was about 24,000 seats. The place
reached capacity since we were playing Duke in-between the
UCLA and Ohio State games.

I walked to half-court for the tip-off and stood face to face
with Shane Battier. He was a senior, and I was only a sophomore,
but he looked like a grown man. He walked around the half-court

circle exchanging pleasantries with us and looking each one of his teammates directly in the eyes before saying, "It starts here!" He walked up to me, nodded his head and said, "Good luck."

Our journeys were wildly different. To us, this game was the biggest one of our lives. To them, we were the initial speed bump on the way to the goal of a National Championship. It was my job to make sure their journey ended here. I had taken responsibility for Shane's success during the previous day's press conference, and I had to go out and give it my best.

The ref entered the circle with the ball. We both bent our knees, extended our hands and prepared to jump.

"The ball was tipped, and there we were.
I was running for my life; I was a shooting star.
And all the years, no one knew,
just how hard I worked, but now it shows.
In one shining moment, it was all on the line.
One shining moment, there frozen in time."

Luther Vandross' voice replayed over and over in my head as we raced up and down the court. I was focused, trying to keep up with the best team in college basketball history. Finally, the ball came to me just a few feet from the basket. I took a step, squared my shoulders and laid it in. I was exhilarated. I fought off a smile as I ran down the court. This feeling was fleeting as I glanced at the scoreboard: Duke-16; Monmouth-3.

While I gave it my all, trying to defend a future NBA lottery pick, Shane's final stat line still read twenty-one points and ten rebounds, which I blame more on the kinks in the zone, which, ironically, I was also primarily responsible for. Although we lost, I still maintain that the game was much closer than the 95-52 score indicated.

After licking my wounds, I was determined to make it back to the NCAA tournament. However, it was not in the cards. Injuries plagued my junior year and, despite a few upsets over top teams, we were not able to reclaim the glory of the past year.

Senior year was a rebuilding year that, while successful for me individually, was not the ending of my collegiate career that I had hoped for but would propel Monmouth to the 2004 NCAA Tournament the year after I graduated.

Like Coach Crawford early in my high school career, my collegiate coaches sat me down at the end of my senior year and asked me if I was serious about playing professional basketball. I gave a far more enthusiastic answer than the one seven years before. My coaches assured me they would help me achieve that goal by any means possible. Unbeknownst to them, I crammed seven straight years of sacrifice, missing out on all the good parts of college like drinking, eating and getting fat, into two and a half months. I showed up to play pickup at the beginning of the summer against the underclassmen. Even though my once model-worthy midsection now resembled Endgame Thor, I still volunteered for our team to go skins. What a mistake! The ten pounds of mass I recently acquired gathered strictly in my stomach. I was out of shape and not sharp. Word got back to the coaches who met me in the gym hallway later that day.

They took one look at me and shook their heads. Although I was no longer under their jurisdiction, they laid into me. It was reminiscent of the angry, hour-long lecture my dad gave me in the parking lot of a 1997 high school summer league game. Pissed that I had not played well and was lackadaisical in my efforts, he let me have it in a now-legendary bit of Camden Catholic folklore. All the negative life choices I had made were ridiculed, as Zahir McGhee and Amir Little, the two teammates we were soon to be giving a ride home to, stood awkwardly a few feet away. I had not lived up to the expectations I was capable of and was called out on it.

The lecture from my coaches hit harder, as I was twenty-two and should have known better. I could see the disappointment in their eyes and knew I owed them more than I was giving. I am eternally grateful for these talks, as they helped refocus my sometimes fun-loving mind. I hit the gym harder than I ever had that summer in hopes of reaching the next level. My coaches had kept true to their promise. They had given me all the guidance I needed to be successful. Once I walked off that campus, it was up to me to complete my sacred quest.

Chapter 2

Exposed

I owe a lot to my brother Geoff. From our early childhood days, when he would punch me in the back as hard as he could when I got out of line or when I upset him, or when he wanted to show his dominance, which he did often. Face punching was outlawed in my household, but back and arm punches were considered fair game. My brother was what we refer to in puberty as a gradual grower, meaning he grew at a steady rate, eventually ending when he reached the 7-foot mark he currently resides at. I, however, grew in large spurts. One day I would resemble a small child, and the next, I was the tallest kid in my class. This cycle repeated itself off and on throughout my adolescence. During these lapses in growth, my brother, who could have passed for my father, asserted his superiority.

One night during a tense game of Nerf basketball, Geoff, who held a commanding 26-4 lead at the time, lowered his shoulder and knocked me through the drywall. My dad ran into our bedroom, worried that someone had been seriously hurt. He opened the door to find my brother yelling at me that I grabbed his arm on the way up, and me, with my ass lodged into the interior workings of the wall, arguing back that it was an obvious charge. His ridiculous size advantage made a small twerp like me easy pickings. Because of his imposing will and all those back punches, not to mention that in my household, telling was a sign of weakness, I was able to take a beating and develop the mental and physical toughness needed for a career in professional basketball.

He was my model of success. I was compared to Geoff often growing up, mainly because he was good at basketball, and I sucked. I admittedly did not take basketball seriously, spending my youth chasing girls and playing with Thundercats. I was constantly behind in both basketball skills and physical development throughout middle school and high school. It took a decade to figure out, but once I did, we evened out.

We were around the same size, same build, and played similar styles of the sport. We were both tough, bruising post players known for our rebounding and maximum effort, which was always on display. All those years of playing together in the driveway allowed us to learn from each other. I was the yin to his yang and vice versa. My brother learned to loosen up and enjoy the fun aspects of life, while I learned to toughen up and take things seriously. I would eventually be called a *try hard* by a frustrated opponent trying to make the team and thought I was playing too aggressively, despite his athletic ability nearly double mine. I ended up getting a contract, and the player ended up released from the team.

But most of all, I owe my professional basketball career to Geoff. Coming out of Monmouth University, I had gained some notoriety. I scored over 1,000 points during my four-year career and had competed in a hard-fought seventeen-second tie with eventual National Champion Duke in the NCAA Tournament. That notoriety, however, did not lead to a spot in the NBA Draft.

Ironically, I was still considered a developing player, coming out of a small school and looking to try my hand at pro basketball. My brother, then a center for the Roanoke Dazzle, a D-League team located in Roanoke, Virginia, had established himself for the same hardworking reputation we had been known for previously. The D-League, which is now referred to as the G-league after Gatorade and the NBA decided that having a true minor league system was something that it should probably be invested in, was only in its second year of existence. Back then, it was still just the D-League or Development League, a place where young borderline NBA talent could compete, make no money, but be seen often by NBA scouts. My agent, Mike Siegel, who also represented my brother, another perk I had being the younger sibling, understandably could not find a foreign team that would take a chance on me, sight unseen. I ended up playing in an exposure camp in hopes of catching the eye of anyone willing to pay me in some sort of currency other than smiles.

Exposure camps are the epitome of undrafted overseas basketball free agent life. Most of the top prospects had already been through Portsmouth or the NBA Draft Combine before being placed into this pool and therefore were on most teams' radar. The overseas exposure camps are for the second, third, fourth, and in my case, twelfth tier guys. It's a group of European scouts and agents who sit in a hot musty gym, in hot musty clothes, smelling hot and musty, while watching basketball players fight for their professional lives.

My first experience at one such camp occurred the summer after my senior year. Even though I once took a charge on Duke University star and All-Time Charge leader Shane Battier, apparently, these coaches needed to see more. So, I hopped into my pickup truck and drove the four and a half hours down to Virginia Commonwealth University to try and turn some heads. Exposure camps are not free. The camp fee, hotel, registration and pleasure to possibly get seen by the right team are paid for out of the player's pocket.

Ideally, agents expense the trip, fly you down first-class, put you up at a swanky hotel and take you out for an expensive dinner. That thought crossed my mind as I parked my pickup truck in an empty spot close to the Arby's and walked into the Hampton Inn to see if the room I would be sharing with a stranger for three days was ready. The attractive woman at the front desk, who had understandably been eye-fucked all day, informed me that my room was not yet ready, and I had to live out of my car for the morning before I reported to the gym.

The camp began like any other organized basketball encounter. We were shuffled together into different groups and informed of the expectations and rules of the camp, in this case, how the 200 individuals that sat around you would be fighting for six or seven total spots. It's reminiscent of the scene in *The Dark Knight*, where The Joker breaks a pool cue and throws the sharp object into the middle of three men, knowing only two can live and the survivors must murder their peer. That is how I felt, not to that extent, but definitely with a sense of fear and apprehension that I would not be good enough and that someone would shove a sharp metaphorical object into my ribs.

Fear was a natural reaction for me. Even from a young age, when I inexplicably thought the werewolf from *Silver Bullet* was climbing up the brick exterior wall into my second-story window to gruesomely kill me, fear tended to cloud my intellect. It is why I have always assumed if I dipped my toes in the ocean, a shark would eat me. In the case of the exposure camp, despite all of my improvements and all of the recognition I received playing college basketball, I feared I would not be good enough. For people like me who tend to overthink things, that nonsensical fear is always there. Whether you are the best player, the CEO, or the little guy trying to make it big, fear comes in and questions everything you are. Am I tall enough, am I strong enough, or am I just plain good enough? The greats in the world experience fear, analyze, and shut it down. But they experience it just like everyone else.

Each of us sat around like an episode of *Survivor*. We waited for the secret package that would reveal our colored jersey and show us who we'd be going through this experience with and against. My name got called for the yellow team, along with nine other names I was not familiar with. We walked into our small groups and introduced ourselves before being given a yellow jersey with a number on the back representing our ranking; 1

being the best and 200 being the worst. I slipped on number 177 to check the fit and began preparing for our first practice. Due to the printing company's tendency to use the largest jerseys for the largest numbers, they handed me an XXXL jersey that hung off my narrow frame like a sweatshirt in the '80s.

Many factors contributed to my professional basketball career. My family played an intricate role, as well as my coaches. And others were simply from the individual plays that made a coach look up and say, "Wow!" Like during my first practice with my new exposure camp team.

Our first practice began with several drills showcasing our skills, one of which, for some reason, being a fast break one-on-one chase drill. This drill is a popular staple amongst basketball coaches, as it provides a combination of sprinting, toughness and finishing at the basket. An offensive player starts slightly ahead of the defender on the baseline. On the coach's whistle, both players take off on a full sprint to the opposite basket. The defender's goal is to stop the opponent's progress with the ball and make a defensive stop.

One of my teammates on Team Yellow was AND1 Mixtape star, John "Helicopter" Humphries. He was known for his ability to jump very high over random people and objects. I somehow got paired up with John after the guy in front of me saw the matchup and decided he needed to tie his shoe. I had watched him throw down a vertical 360 with as much effort as it took me to hold a pencil earlier that day, but my shot at a job was on the line, so I stepped up. John took off down the floor. I accelerated after him like a lion chasing down prey. I was somehow keeping up with him as we raced down the court. Everything around me became a blur. I could see that I had a good angle to meet him at the basket and block his shot. John, however, had not even acknowledged my existence as he locked eyes on the rim and took off, ironically, like a helicopter. I took off more like an ostrich, my oversized gold jersey nearly engulfing my being, as I went to block the shot of one of the best leapers in the world. It was around that time when I realized what a colossal mistake I had made.

I jumped as high as I could. John jumped higher. We met at the rim, and our bodies crashed into each other like two rams trying to impress a sheep. I heard the distinct sound of the coils of the retractable rim snapping down and then back up, followed by the screaming of three hundred people who were all now celebrating my demise. I had been dunked on, dunked on bad.

I flashed back to the first time I had been dunked on in a Sonny Hill League game in my sophomore year in high school. I was playing up on my brother's team, as that was a thing we did back then. I saw him out of the corner of my eye. He had been manhandling us all day, hitting shots, snatching rebounds and living up to the hype that surrounded him the past few years. He caught the ball on the wing and baited the defender to the left before crossing it back to his right. He took off down the lane like Rocksteady from the *Teenage Mutant Ninja Turtles*. He was an unstoppable force, and I was an extremely movable object. Being the foolish child I was at the time, I jumped to try and create some sort of deterrence. But to no avail. He dunked on me with such force I needed a few seconds to remember where I was. I jumped and was posterized by arguably the best basketball player the planet has ever seen, Kobe Bryant.

As I jogged back into line for Team Yellow, I tried to maintain my game face despite the humiliation of being dunked on, again, this time, by a Helicopter. After getting embarrassed in front of forty-two musty scouts, a handful of workers, and the 198 other players in attendance, I was pretty sure it was over for me. When our practice ended, I opted not to check into my hotel room to hide. I did not know my roommate, and I didn't want to find out who he was. The impact of that dunk was felt far and wide. If social media existed back then, I would have been a meme. The person I'd be sharing a room with was going to ask me questions, or tell me I sucked, or even worse, not say a word and just smirk. He would probably identify me as the guy who got dunked on (I didn't know at the time that I would be known as the guy who interrupted the orgy). I had no interest in any of those interactions. Therefore I decided to stay at the gym and watch the following practice game from the stands.

I took out my backpack and pulled out the sad lunch of peanut butter and jelly I had packed. I only had funds to dine out one meal per day. One tall scout with a grey beard and a dark tan walked up to me as I finished my last bit of crust. "Are you Kevin Owens?" he asked me.

Uh oh, they figured out who I was. Now he's going to give me a pep talk about how the world needs tall teachers. I timidly responded, "Yes."

I was certain he was simply verifying my name for the video that would lead off *SportsCenter* the next morning. Instead, he looked me in the eyes and said, "It took lots of guts to challenge Humphries. You keep a strong mentality, and you will be a success."

Life suddenly made sense again. My confidence had been restored. I could see the looks from other players who thought they could *helicopter* me. I felt the fear, analyzed it and shut it down. Throughout the day, I played against players from high-level universities. I quickly realized, where you went to college no longer mattered. I was outplaying guys that went to Miami, Indiana and Connecticut. I left the arena that evening with a whole new level of confidence and a sense of relief. That is until I arrived at the hotel and was greeted by the sexual extravaganza I previously described.

I finished out the week strong, even making the All-Star Game. I proved that living out of your truck was kind of like camping and having zero money motivates you a whole lot more than I thought. I got an excited call from my agent a few weeks later. I proved myself talented enough at the exposure camp to warrant an invite to the 2003 D-League Draft.

The D-League Draft was an invite-only affair. Only sixty players were extended an invitation. Additionally, another sixty players who had D-League experience who were already rostered by a team were also invited. A total of 120 athletes flew down to

Atlanta, Georgia, for medical testing, seminars and meetings. I packed enough clothing to last seven months, despite knowing I may only need enough for nineteen days: three in Atlanta, fourteen for training camp and one more for the flight home after my ass was cut. Over the next few days, I was poked and prodded by coaches and trainers who tried to determine if I was D-League material. My brother, already comfortably on a team, shared a room with me during this nerve-wracking process and did his best to make me believe I did not suck, that I actually had a chance.

The night of the draft, I sat in my hotel room waiting for a phone call; the 2003 D-League Draft wasn't televised, broadcast or cared about by anyone but the draft hopefuls and maybe their families. During the middle of the 8th Round, my hotel phone rang. I answered in anticipation only to hear, "Is Geoff there?"

What the hell?! Even at this moment, he's getting phone calls. However, Geoff was not taking a social call. It was Kent Davison, the coach of the Roanoke Dazzle, telling him they were going to draft me, but also, unless I impressed him, Geoff would have to be ok if they cut me. As Geoff was deemed important, it was a courtesy call; the team did not want to upset him by cutting me. The content of this conversation was a mystery to me at this point. There was no emotion on my brother's face, just the occasional nod. He smiled at me and passed me the phone.

"Kevin," the raspy voice began, "this is Kent Davison. I coach the Roanoke Dazzle. We are drafting you with our next pick. Congratulations!"

I wish I said something professional, but the only word my shocked mouth could muster was, "Cool!" I thanked him for the confidence and hung up the phone. I had been selected in the 8th Round of the NBA Development League Draft. I would be playing alongside Geoff in Roanoke, Virginia, officially starting my pro career.

The Dazzle had the tough distinction of being close to Virginia Tech and considered second-rate. The D-League had that perception. People assumed that you would go directly to the

NBA and become a star if you were a highly rated college basketball player. If you weren't, you would move on and get a job like any other N.A.R.P. (Non-Athletic Regular People.) At that time, the D-League was new. People didn't have a good understanding of it. To them, any good college team would smack us around since we were the NBA rejects.

It was never more apparent than my first preseason game with the Roanoke Dazzle. I was on the fringe of making the team when we arrived at The Comcast Center against the future ACC Champ Maryland Terrapins, aka the Terps. It was their last preseason game before they would begin the season with a Top 25 ranking. We were the outcasts, not an NBA team, not an overseas team and not a college team. We were something else in their eyes.

Over 4,000 college basketball players are draft eligible each year, with only sixty slots available. Thirty of those slots are guaranteed, and between ten to twenty of those sixty slots are foreign players. Only 1.2% of all players get drafted and only .7% make an NBA roster. Maintaining a multiple-year NBA career is even more difficult, as this cycle repeats itself every year and the number on an NBA roster does not change. This means the players making up a D-League team all had NBA experience in some capacity. We could all be on the end of an NBA bench if maybe we had a different agent, a different coach in college, or you were not man-humped by one of the best defensive players in NBA history while trying to make the team an event that occurred later in my career. We were good, really good. The scary thing was, we knew that, but they didn't.

It was a packed house in the Comcast Center that night. Maryland's student section, notorious for their treatment of opposing teams, was in full force as they prepared for their regular season, starting just a few days later. Twenty minutes before game time and the place was rocking. 50 Cent was blasting over the speakers, the crowd was raucous, and I was taking the court for the first time as a professional basketball player.

At this time in my life, I was out of college, had played the game and done the clean-cut thing for a while. But now, I was an adult and could present myself in any way I wanted. My hair had grown considerably long, and I embraced those long flowing locks by dying them blonde. Because of my hair and the fact that I was a tall, goofy white guy, I became an instant target. The entire student section focused all their efforts on destroying my life.

Whenever you hear stories of athletes not hearing what fans are saying because they are so focused or good at ignoring people, it is absolute bullshit. You hear everything, Every! Fucking! Thing! No matter how focused you are, you hear every word. Your ability to block it out and not let it get to you separates the mentally tough from the not mentally tough. That evening, I heard everything.

"CUT YOUR HAIR SOLDIER," a random student shouted. "THIS IS WARTIME!"

"YOU WILL NOT MAKE THIS SHOT! YOU JACKASS!!!" an overly large individual belted out.

"I CAN'T BELIEVE YOU ARE A PROFESSIONAL BASKETBALL PLAYER!" a voice from the top row screamed. "YOU LOOK LIKE YOU SHOULD BE WORKING IN THE SNACK BAR!" Happy Gilmore was still a big thing at this point.

Every time I caught the ball, 2,000 students screamed the most obscene insults they could think of my way. Weirdly, it pumped me up. I remember thinking that I must have been important. That they knew who I was, and they knew if they got to me, they would win.

Now that I am older and wiser, I knew they didn't think that way. That they only looked at me as someone to humiliate for their drunken enjoyment. I really should say thank you to them or send a care package to the Maryland student section filled with prescription drugs and Axe body spray or whatever the fuck college kids find so cool these days. These fans gave me the confidence to go out and dominate, giving my coach the confidence to offer me a contract. At one point, I had the most magnificent tip dunk of my career over half of the Maryland team. I remember running right past the group of fans who had insulted my mother, girlfriend, dog, hair and socks, and stared them down like Kobe. I looked over shortly after, and the seats were empty. I assumed the students went back to paddling each other's asses and shotgunning Natty Lights.

That evening was the greatest achievement of my young career. Everything rode on that game. My career, my journey, the friends and teammates I would meet and even this book. My entire basketball future lived or died with that one game. And I straight up DOMINATED! I had walked into a small high school gym in Roanoke, Virginia, two weeks before with nothing to lose and everything to gain and walked out with my first professional contract.

Coach Kent Davison informed me that when he called my brother that fateful Draft day, he told him that I would most likely be cut. My brother never said a word, just hung up the phone, smiled and told me to dominate! I obliged. Without Geoff, I never would have been invited to the D-League Draft. He got my foot into the door; I kicked that bitch down.

Chapter 3

The D/G-League

The smell of eggs, bacon and hash browns marinated the air as I sipped on my coffee.

"Top it off, Hun?" Joan, our seventy-two-year-old waitress, asked as I nodded my head and smiled. She treated us like we were her children. Over the past few months, we had developed that close relationship. I didn't know her last name or anything about her life other than the fact that she worked late nights at The Waffle House in Roanoke and that her evening was complete when my teammate Seth Doliboa and I would pop in for a late-night omelet. These trips were a necessary evil for us. As embracing the interactions with the community and trying our best to keep from losing weight with the rigors of the NBA D-League season, trumped sitting alone in an empty apartment. Seth and I had developed a brotherly relationship, making the Joan, Seth and Kevin family dynamic complete.

Seth was from Ohio and a hard-working blue-collar family, while my like-minded family hailed from the Philadelphia area. He attended Wright State University, a small Division 1 academic institution, before joining the D-League with the

Columbus Riverdragons. We had other similarities as well. Seth was recently acquired by my team, the Roanoke Dazzle, just a few days after being released by Columbus. He was a victim of the biggest issue with professional basketball: being twice the player but half the name. You see, being a late bloomer was very difficult for guys like Seth and me. I had the muscle mass and metabolism of an eighth-grader when I was a senior in college. I competed against guys who were the finished product of their maturation, while the smallest bit of facial hair barely peeked out from under my nose. My one roommate used to shave his back due to the excessive amounts of hair encompassing his body, while I still had yet to grow any hair on my chest. These biological limitations led me to Monmouth University, a small school where I was recruited based on potential.

I am not sure why, but for some reason, while I slowly matured, the rest of the world appeared to be aging in some sort of dog-year system. That was until shortly after I turned twenty-three years old, when my delayed puberty took off. I suddenly sprouted muscles and gained weight, something I had a hard time achieving, despite a similar work ethic, in college. I found myself as strong as my peers who had spent so long pushing me around. Like a fine wine, my body continued to grow better with age. While most athletes hit their prime in their mid to late twenties, I continually improved into my thirties. Still to this day, I am not sure what my internal clock reads. Each year, I grow stronger and more handsome.

My skill set and work ethic, combined with my manly metamorphosis, propelled me ahead of many of the competitors I would face in professional basketball. The only problem, despite my rise in talent and strength, I still was just a kid from Monmouth. My new Captain America body, while impressive, could not compete with my reputation as a frail, skinny kid. Players who were lucky enough to develop at the tender age of sixteen years old had the stigma of a big-name school and were put in higher regard than us late bloomers.

Seth and I shared this reputation and relished any opportunity to prove that where you went to college no longer mattered. Our juvenescent prime and similar upbringings were discussed as we stretched together a week into Seth's tenure with the team. We became friends shortly after. It only took a few practices, some team dinners, and one crazy bus ride back from the club, where we witnessed unthinkable debauchery involving trash bags, a willing woman participant and the back of a crowded bus. That is what brought us to this Waffle House on a late Tuesday evening in January.

I glanced at my primitive cell phone, which read two o'clock in the morning. We had just hopped off the bus from a short four-hour trip from Fayetteville, North Carolina, after a back-to-back home/away matchup with the Fayetteville Patriots. It was our fourth game against them in thirteen days. With only six teams in the league and forty-eight regular-season games, trips like this became the norm, as did late-night trips to the Waffle House after these long bus rides.

I tipped a mug of coffee back and took a large mouthful of Royal Cup, ignoring the caffeine boost that would keep me up for the next three hours. I had slept on the bus, and with a day off coming, I knew I had plenty of time to rest. I could see Joan had my order nearly complete and ran to the bathroom before my two o'clock in the morning protein boost. One of the twelve random truckers we shared the small restaurant with stopped me as I walked by. Enamored with my height, and delusional from his caffeine and Snickers-induced stupor, he grabbed my arm and exclaimed, "You tall as shit! Is the fuckin' circus in town?!"

I was shocked. I have heard every tall joke, question, or comment known to man. It is one of the side effects of being gigantic. It appears people are extremely comfortable approaching a large man and asking personal questions about their life. You will never see this with any other interaction known to man. People do not walk up to a fat person and ask them how much they weigh or if their parents were also obese. Short people are not asked if they are a jockey. But with tall people, it is open season for fuckery.

One time while walking through Walmart during my rookie year in Roanoke, a man approached my 7-foot brother, my 7-foot teammate Josh Asselin and me. In typical redneck fashion, he began the three steps of what I called the redneck circus, an event occurring when a redneck encountered anyone taller than 5-feet 11-inches.

There was the initial "Holy Shit!" in front of his seven children, all suspiciously under the age of six. Then the peacocking as he strutted around next to us, jumping up and down, pretending he was our size. Finally, what I like to refer to as Redneck Jeopardy consists of a bombardment of dumbass questions.

"Yes, there is a butt-ton of traffic in New Jersey."

"No, I do not follow Nascar."

Or just a subtle observation. As I stood in line with Geoff and Josh and the man asked the three of us, dead serious, "Y'all twins?"

Instead of giving this genetically challenged specimen an explanation of what the word *twins* meant, I smiled, replied "Yes," and continued on my way. For some reason, when you are tall, people assume you are up for an interrogation. Maybe they admire us, or maybe they are jealous, or maybe they think being tall and athletic is lame. But this night, this night at the Waffle House...this was different.

Seth sprang from his seat, fist balled, looking to beat the ever-living shit out of this mouthy Jabba the Hutt clone. Seth was more aggressive than I was and never backed down; I was more passive, choosing to defuse tense situations instead of engaging in full-on combat. Seth was already there.

"What did you say, you fucking bitch?" Seth yelled in his distinct Northeastern Ohio accent. I ripped my arm away from the sweaty sausage fingers that grasped around me and stood in front of Seth, blocking him from the confrontation. "That is how you are going to talk to another human being? Look at you. Look at your gut!"

The overweight truck driver quickly stood up like he was David about to take down Goliath. Unfortunately for him, the biblical tale where the small inferior human took down the giant had a different outcome. Maybe it was because he was older, or maybe his body was not accustomed to anything other than long mileage driving, but when he whirled out of his seat, gravity pulled him right back to earth, and he toppled over onto the syrup-soaked Waffle House floor.

I quickly pushed Seth back to our seats as he laughed at the misfortune of our aggressor. The man was helped to his feet by several similar-bodied truckers and escorted out the door. Before he reached the exit, he turned to us and yelled, "The Dazzle Suck! Y'all can't make the NBA because y'all suck! No one comes to your games cause no one cares!"

It all came out. An honest opinion of what most people thought of the D-League. That we were not good enough, and no number of wins against top collegiate teams was going to change it. While I was aware, he did not speak for the entire world, his words still resonated. The thought that I was in a dead-end job began swirling through my mind. I don't understand. This was the D-League! We were just a phone call away from playing in the NBA. How could anyone look down on us? How could anyone look down upon this league? We were affiliated with the Philadelphia 76ers, Charlotte Bobcats and the Washington Wizards, for Christ's sake! But that was the overwhelming feeling about our professional organization and us.

I find myself constantly defending the D-League to random strangers, even to this day. As with the near brawl at the local Waffle House, most interactions start with the usual, "How tall are you?" in a polite, or in the latter case, not so nice way. Followed by "Do or did you play basketball? Where did you play?"

This inquiry is particularly humbling since I am not famous enough to be recognized, at least not in the United States.

I start by going through the list. A little here in America in the D-League, a cup of coffee in the NBA, or in my case, an espresso, then I list the menagerie of countries I was employed in. The person at this point is intrigued. They thought they were just grabbing a quick cup of coffee from the local Wawa, and they ended up meeting an International Man of Mystery. I've fictitiously kept a pie chart over the years of the random conversations I've had regarding my playing days. I've noticed the conversation usually steers toward the D-League.

"Did you enjoy playing in the D-League?" a person always asks.

"Yes!" I exclaim with great empathy.

"Really? I heard most players hated it." An additional cross-examination ensues. "Did you have anyone at your games? Heard the pay was horrible." Or the occasional jackass, who thinks playing in the D-League is comparable to playing in their local men's league.

The negative connotation of the D-League is not limited to just fans. Former players have been opinionated on their experiences as well. Many are frustrated by the lousy pay, small towns and rigorous travel on Coach buses. The D-League is like playing in the NBA except for one glaring difference: the meager salary and the small towns most teams are located in. NBA stars pull in one of the highest salaries in sports, while as a rookie in the D-League, the starting salary, at least when I played, was just $12,000 for the year. Imagine being on the fringe of the NBA and you are pulling in less than a substitute teacher. The fringe NBA player reputation is great until the season ends, and you have to move back into your parent's attic for the summer. That sort of lifestyle doesn't exactly scream Baller.

I'm never surprised by the abundance of former D-Leaguers who look down on their experiences. For me, as a young player coming out of college, playing for this organization was the most influential period of my life. The D-League itself is a very humbling experience. Being so close to the glitz and glam of the NBA, but in these small towns, feeling so very far away.

My first year in the D-League was a wild experience. To be honest, I had no idea what I was doing. I did not know anything. I was just happy to be there. My professional basketball start was a lot like the original Super Mario Brothers. The levels started out easy and would become increasingly more difficult. Every time I had a little victory and reached the end of one stage, leaping as high as I could on that weird flagpole, I would breathe a sigh of relief, only to be met by the start of the next level where some asshole in a cloud throws an endless supply of hammers at me. That was my first year as a pro basketball player. I had made it through the exposure camp, which got me an invite to the D-League. I then had to fight off twelve other players to make the ten-man roster, only to fight those ten players for playing time every day in practice. Eventually, I realized that I was in some kind of Thunderdome, fighting off not only my opponents but my teammates as well. Especially when one of them was a similar size, similar position, and also had a similar last name, Geoff Owens.

Having two brothers both make it this far in professional basketball during the early 2000s was unheard of. This was before the injection of superhuman basketball families like the Holiday and Curry brothers, the Morris and Lopez twins, and the whole Zeller crew. At that time, we were it: Two brothers who shared the same uniform, same court and same basketball dream, well, sort of.

Our dreams at the time were slightly different. I was insanely proud that I had made it to the D-League and the label of pro basketball player. I had fought with all my might, and I was happy, maybe even a little content. However, my brother, after just finishing a training camp stint with the Cleveland Cavaliers, where he shared a court with a popular rookie by the name of LeBron James, was pushing for the next step.

If ever there was a barometer of our two differentiating personalities, it showed when we were introduced to the world during the once-popular NBC show, *NBA Inside Stuff*, which gave a weekly recap of the NBA season and provided the behind-the-scenes stories of professional basketball. Maybe it was because I was a rookie, but I had a very nonchalant attitude to this news. Thinking back, I was like a deer in headlights during my rookie year. Everything was new, everything was unique, and I guess I just looked at this as another experience. I was in such a daze that I did not even tell my friends I would be appearing. This was before social media, where I could blast news like this out to everyone and watch as my likes and ego grow. I was not nervous; I was just there in the moment, not thinking about the next step, but simply enjoying every day.

The crew came a few weeks later and set up in our locker room. I remember spending a great deal of time on my hair, despite what you might have seen during the final cut. We put on our jerseys and sat side by side, answering questions about growing up, playing together, brotherly love and other feel-good topics. Then the question of the NBA came up.

"The NBA is always in the back of your mind," I responded.

"Sometimes it's in the front of your mind," my brother interrupted.

Oh, Shit I thought, as my nationally televised aha moment became apparent. *This is why I am here, I repeated to myself. This is not the final step or culmination of my journey but another stepping stone. The NBA is my goal.* I do not know why it took me so long to put this all into perspective, but it was the first time I realized my true purpose in the D-League. NBA scouts saw eighty players daily, and I was one of them. And to make matters more stressful, one of my competitors for an NBA contract was sitting right next to me. I needed a reboot. I was playing games like I had done my whole life, with the focus of winning and not necessarily selling myself as a player. I was here for a reason and needed to utilize my teammates not just as aids in a group effort to win but as guides to what I needed to improve on.

I spent the better part of the year under the tutelage of two notable NBA veterans: Cory Alexander and Mikki Moore. They gave me a crash course in leadership and how to take care of my body during a long grueling season. Mikki told me that my effort and hustle made me who I am, but I needed to find time in the game to relax and refocus, or I would burn myself out. He taught me that I need to occasionally slow down and not always play the game at ludicrous speed. Cory was a tremendous point guard and leader. He was great at being a spokesman for the team, teaching us all how to handle the press and how to be a pro both on and off the floor.

Josh Asselin, a 6-foot 11-inch Michigan alum, helped me perfect my spin move, which gave me much success as I progressed in my career. On the first day of training camp, I tried to muscle the 6-foot 11-inch forward off the post, by applying pressure with my forearm into his back and shifting my weight from my heels to my toes in the hope that he would be forced to take a difficult shot. Josh, no stranger to this move, accepted my shift of weight, forcing me off balance before leveraging his elbow into my arm while quickly spinning towards the basket for a one-handed dunk. Josh would use this move at least 276 times during the season on many other unsuspecting defenders who thought the same as me. Josh proved that brains will always beat brawn.

Along with my new teammates, my oldest and most familiar teammate continued to teach me. I learned how to handle the physicality of professional basketball from Geoff, whose temper sometimes got the best of him. One practice, he got into a shoving match with our 7-foot 2-inch Danish center Chris Christoffersen and nearly came to blows before I jumped in and threatened Chris' life. Chris was twice my size, noticeably taller, and also my roommate at the time. Geoff and I also had our share of physical altercations when paired up against each other at practice, bringing us back to our youth. These were much more psychologically damaging as these battles weren't over baseball cards or video games, but million-dollar contracts, fame and an eternal legacy of being an NBA player.

I gained a great deal of basketball knowledge from my coach, Kent Davison. Mainly the phrase, "What have you done for me lately?" and "If it was easy, everyone would do it." But mainly his wise words of describing how to get to the NBA, "You are not going to the NBA to be a superstar, find that one thing you are good at, and be the best at it." For me, that was rebounding, and I was pretty fucking good at it.

On SpongeBob SquarePants night, I learned that our arena would be packed with young children who gave zero fucks about what we were doing on the court and a million fucks about the guy dressed in a giant foam Spongebob costume. After the halftime show, the crowd would clear out, leaving just the usual crowd of around 400 who, while small in size, were the most loyal fans around.

I learned that Christmas dinner at a gas station in Fayetteville, North Carolina, is as depressing as it sounds, as are eighteen-hour bus rides and connecting flights. Also, when the employees of Roanoke Convention Center say you need to leave so they can set up for the rodeo, you need to get out quickly as the animals are the first to be unloaded.

I learned the only one responsible for my overall improvement was me. Attending optional shoot arounds and staying late after practice were not options, but requirements if an NBA contract was the goal; being tired was not an excuse.

The D-League has a forty-eight-game schedule played within five months. There are no games for rest or load management. We don't play, we don't get seen. Not being seen means no chance of an NBA call-up. This means playing through pain and floor burns, and diving into the stands for a loose ball is necessary. I learned that success was not how many points you scored but rather how hard you hustled and how hard you worked.

But most of all, I learned humility. Whether from the semi-pro dance team member who still performed during timeouts while seven months pregnant, or the invitation to a birthday party of a young fan, which we graciously accepted, you are brought down to earth pretty quickly.

The following summer, I committed another year to the D-League. Although I had gained a great deal of knowledge, I knew I still had a long way to go. I arrived at training camp officially a *veteran*. In the off-season, I had bulked up quite a bit (steroid-free). I knew that for me to start, I needed to be stronger.

I was met by a 7-foot power forward out of Iowa State who walked up to me in the hotel lobby before the first practice and introduced himself as the starting power forward of the Roanoke Dazzle. I never got rattled by shit-talking like that. I just buried it deep inside my anger bank and went all Incredible Hulk when I stepped on the floor. Again, I walked into that small high school gym with a chip on my shoulder. I walked out the starting power forward for an extremely talented Roanoke Dazzle. We had several Gatorade Call Ups that year, including my roommate Matt Carroll, who held an NBA contract seven years after his time in the D-League.

Spoiler Alert: the dude from Iowa State was cut.

My second year in Roanoke was also my best shot at the NBA. My brother had left for a contract in France, and I was able to flourish on my own. I spent practices working with my assistant coach and former NBA journeyman Chucky Brown. He taught me how to better position myself for rebounds and utilize my forearms on defense. The advice helped me become one of the top rebounders in the League. During that year, I realized how much I improved since this journey began. A realization shared by my agent Mike Siegel, who, after watching me play one night for the first time in months, told me, "Wow, you got good!" While it was flattering, I could not help but think that if he thought I was really good before that, I might have been waving a towel at the end of an NBA bench.

The following summer, I decided that, although I loved the D-League and appreciated every aspect, it was time to make some money off this game. I received a contract from a team in Poland and stayed there for a short while until the money dried up (more on that later). Upon returning home, I received a call from my Dazzle teammate and good friend, Seth Doliboa. He convinced me to come back to Roanoke for one more year.

Unfortunately for me, this was the first year that NBA players could be assigned to D-League teams. And as luck would have it, both players sent down from the Washington Wizards played the same position as I did. I was forced to sit the bench. I made the most of my demotion and continued to work hard competing against young NBA players Andre Blatche and Peter John Ramos every day at practice. I finished up the season frustrated but excited for my future abroad.

I often reflect on the D-League, mainly referring to the question I'd been asked so many times, "Did you enjoy playing in the D-League?"

And despite my last season's frustrations, the answer was still a resounding, "Yes!" Most people would call me crazy. Most people would say the D-League is a punishment. And that stigma is something I completely understand.

Indulge me if you will. Imagine being an NBA rookie. You are told how amazing you are throughout your life. You are a superstar at a high-end Division 1 university where you are given everything you need before declaring for the draft. You are then drafted, sign a lucrative contract and enjoy all the bells and whistles that go along with it. Suddenly your coach and GM appear, sit you down in their office and say that you will be sent down to the minors to *develop*.

You are then shipped to a small town whose idea of Saturday night fun is a bar named Corned Beef (100% true). You practice in an elementary school gym, which was used for a P.T.A. meeting the night before. Occasionally you have to drive a half-hour to practice because your gym is being used for an eighth-grade dance. You end up waiting until a forty-three-year-old periodontist finishes with the forty-pound weights so you can finish your set at the local YMCA. As you can imagine, after living the NBA life, it's a bit of a culture shock.

But for me, the D-League was perfect. It was a chance to show off my skills in front of a horde of NBA scouts. It was a chance to develop against some amazing competition. And finally, it was an opportunity to truly appreciate professional basketball. Now I know a lot of prima donnas think the D-League is below them. Most of them think that twelve-hour trips from small-town America to small-town America may be a waste of their time, but the way I see it, even Jordan rode the bus.

Chapter 4

Taste of the Big Time

When I was a kid, we affectionately referred to a specific group of teenagers as The Dudes. They rocked razor-sharp mullets and leather jackets and chased my brothers and me out of the woods across the street from our home. It must have been protected land as houses sat on either side of this three-acre wide plot, yet the woods remained undisturbed. It became our little oasis in the neighborhood. We would spend our weekends together, starting in the spring, mowing out trails, and creating bike jumps. We would come home filthy, and my mom would sit my brother down and check him for ticks. This usually ended with a pack of matches, a pair of tweezers and several band-aids.

These woods became our sanctuary. We would spend several weekends creating the trails and the remainder of the summer racing our bikes. Occasionally we came across a Playboy or some kind of magazine with a far raunchier arrangement of pictures. Coors Light cans would litter the trails on Saturday mornings, and we would toss them in a bag to trade in for candy on our vacations in August. These discoveries allowed us to infer that an older element of humanity existed in these woods.

Each summer, we would stay in the woods on some random day until the sunlight no longer illuminated the trails. On these summer evenings, we would hear the faint sound of chains, spokes and cursing becoming gradually louder and louder until The Dudes were upon us. We would hop on our bikes and head to the closest exit, trying to avoid being snatched up by one of these troubled youths.

Occasionally one of us would be chased away by this group of Huffy's. We would escape overall unscathed, with maybe a cut or two from hopping on our bikes too quickly and plotted our revenge, which entailed stealing their porn mags. The material would either be thrown into the sewer or buried deep into the terrain (I was ten years old at the time and still believed girls had cooties).

One day we decided to amp up our juvenile revenge to something more sinister. As you wound around the final loop of the bike trail, there was a long straightaway leading to a large mound of dirt where we would try to replicate the small, pixelated man from Nintendo's Excitebike and catch as much air as possible. We decided to dig a large hole right in front of the grand finale jump. We covered it with sticks and leaves and anything else we could find to hide the hole, as our guide to mischief at the time was Ernest P. Worrell. We then waited for the familiar chorus of The Dudes entering the woods. Around dusk, they arrived and took their typical victory lap through the bike path. The leader of the group was a real charmer named Dave. He always led the lap and would be the first to reach our cleverly designed booby trap. We watched from behind a tree on the outskirts of the woods.

In typical Dave fashion, he hit the final turn and pedaled as hard as his overly hairy legs could pedal. He made his way closer and closer, faster and faster, until CRASH!! His front tire plummeted into the hole. He went flying into the large mound face first, awkwardly laying there screaming in agony. The remaining Dudes stood in absolute silence, examining his injuries and slowly uncovering the plot against their leader. The faint sound of our giggling caused the group to turn their attention towards our hiding spot. Dave leaped to his feet, wiped the mud off his face, revealing the large amounts of acne strewn about, and glared our way. Hearing the girlish laughs of his prey, he hopped on his bike and pointed in our direction. Instead of staying in our safe hiding spots, we screamed, hopped on our bikes, and got the hell out of there. This turned out to be a huge mistake.

It took The Dudes just seconds to hunt us down and surround us. Geoff had the unfortunate distinction of being extremely tall for his age, making these bullies believe that he was a peer and not an innocent pre-teen just trying to jump a mound of dirt without crashing and breaking an arm. We sat in my neighbor's driveway. Dave began questioning us about our involvement in his faceplant. Every wrong answer meant Geoff got a punch to the stomach. I scanned the neighborhood for a parent, who might have found it odd to see a group of high school kids punching a sixth-grader in the stomach repeatedly. Unfortunately, this was 1990, and parents encouraged this sort of behavior as *learning opportunities*. If this happened today, parents would be filing harassment charges and posting aggressive social media announcements lambasting the parents and the neighbors and probably the police for not being *there* to save Geoff's internal organs from the wrath of a madman.

That was not the case as my brother stood doubled over while the sadistic Dave continued his onslaught of questions. Much like Ralphie in the *Christmas Story,* I felt the rage building inside of me. I grew angrier with every punch to my brother's midsection. Finally, I snapped and screamed, "I DUG THE HOLE!" followed by something like "YOU FART FACE!" or some other insult from my elementary repertoire.

Dave's eyes became red with rage. His attention immediately became focused on me. "Now you pay," he muttered as he approached me.

I had to think fast. One of the oppressors had long shaggy hair and seemed to be keeping watch—we will call him Karl. I seized the moment and kicked Karl in the shin. I pedaled through the escape route as fast as my little legs could carry me. My younger step-brother, interestingly enough, also named Jeff, had been holding a stick throughout this entire encounter. I assumed he would try and whack one of these clowns with it but seeing as Geoff had taken seven to eight punches to the gut at this point, the stick had an ulterior motive.

Dave and his band of goons hopped on their bikes to begin their pursuit. Just as they were about to pedal after me, my younger brother tossed the stick into the spokes of Dave's bike, causing him to flip over his handlebars for the second time in a matter of minutes. The remainder of his group was taken down by this accident. We peddled away as quickly as possible. We reached our house, threw our bikes down and ran inside to safety.

We peaked our heads out of the window as The Dudes, now sporting scraped knees and bloody elbows, circled the street in front of the house like sharks. It was like a scene from the cult classic *The Warriors* as The Dudes just waited for us to come out and play-ay. That is until my 6-foot 7-inch 250-pound father pulled up and gave them a look. They took off in fear and were never heard from again.

Well, almost never. Years later, I would see 5-foot 8-inch overweight bald Dave at a bar. I walked up to him, asked if he remembered me, dipped my finger in his beer, and flicked the suds in his face while calling him a "Fuck Face," or some other insult from my grown-up repertoire.

My ability to hold my own against bigger stronger opposition, led me to PCOM (Philadelphia College of Osteopathic Medicine), aka the practice facility of the Philadelphia 76ers, with a shot of playing for my hometown team. I was fortunate enough to be invited to train with the team I pretended to be a part of in my driveway every day since I was seven years old. I had a workout with them earlier in the summer and performed well enough to be invited back.

The first workout was a tryout for a prospective NBA assistant coach and another random player. I was a test subject for the coach to poke and prod in hopes he would be able to join the staff. We were put through various drills as the coach casually glanced at his notecard to make sure we were thoroughly tortured. 76ers Head Coach at the time, Maurice Cheeks, sat on the sidelines diligently watching. I knew it wasn't just a tryout for the coach, but for us as well. I was on that day, hitting jump shots, making my threes, and even showing off my quasi-athletic jumping ability with some powerful dunks. Afterward, I spoke to a few coaches who fed me compliments, told me I was continuing to improve from my days in the D-League when they had previously watched me and that I would be hearing from them soon. *Holy Shit, they are going to sign me to a guaranteed contract,* I thought, maintaining the overly optimistic attitude I have always harbored.

Flash forward a month, and I still had yet to receive any correspondence from the 76ers. Every time my cell phone rang, I jumped across the couch like Chandler from *Friends*, praying that it was the call I'd been waiting twenty years for. Most of the time, it was my stupid loved ones trying to maintain a positive relationship or asking me to do stuff. After a month of disappointment and disrespect to my inner circle, my agent finally called. The 76ers had invited me back! This was it, the opportunity I had waited for my whole life.

Being that I was a free agent at the time and would be fighting for a job opportunity, I was not given the high-profile free agent treatment. Instead, I found a metered parking spot and walked a few blocks to the athletic center. I had been in the practice facilities of both the Atlanta Hawks and Charlotte Bobcats in the past and experienced the elaborate high-class NBA setup. The Sixers facility was different.

PCOM was a small university for aspiring doctors who shared its campus with the historic professional basketball team.

The facility was about the size of a high school gym, with one full-size NBA court and a small area on the sidelines for storage. I was ushered downstairs by the Equipment Manager and through the weight room used by students who may eventually be my primary care doctor. On the far side of the room was a large door that read Philadelphia 76ers. A passcode was put in, the door buzzed, and I entered the locker room of my heroes. The Iverson era 76ers logo adorned the carpet and walls. Huge wood lockers circled the large room with names like Iguodala, Brand and Williams in large bold letters on top.

"Take that empty locker," he told me, pointing to the empty stretch of openings in the corner. "I'll get your gear."

I sat down and looked around at the room that Hall of Famers sat in before me. The manager walked in with my practice gear and laid it down on my lap. I held up the jersey and stared at it with a shit-eating grin on my face for several minutes before Lou Williams walked in saying, "What's up?" Then he gave me a look like he caught me doing something weird, which he did.

I sat in the locker room putting on my Sixers practice gear, a dream of mine since I met Charles Barkley in the hallway of the Spectrum when I was in sixth-grade. I stood up and looked in the mirror. Realizing how close I was to making an NBA roster, I smiled a confident smile at my reflection, winked and then made my way to the door.

Suddenly *he* appeared behind me, like a shark out of the depths, ready to rip my world apart. But it wasn't an oceanic predator that lurked behind me. Instead, stood thirteen-year NBA vet, Reggie Evans. He was lining me up for a basketball version of a feeding frenzy. Now I know what you are thinking...*Reggie Evans??!! But he's not good!*

Well...A) Are you trying to make me cry?!! Thanks! I think I just died a little inside. And B) If you played that long in the NBA, you are really, really good. And if you are one of the best defenders at that time, you are astronomically good.

I made my way up to the court and hopped into some 1-1 drills with the bigs—no doubt a tough way to start the day, considering my competition. I was in a group with Maurice Speights, Cory Underwood and Elton Brand. I must say I was a little starstruck. That usually does not happen to me, but Elton Brand was a hero of mine since his days dominating Cameron Indoor. On top of being a successful NBA player, Elton Brand was one of the most professional guys in the game. I was an unheard-of, unsigned free agent who should have been treated like a nobody. Elton, a two-time NBA All-Star, took the time to make me feel welcome and offered me some advice on my game. Brand also made me realize why NBA superstars are NBA superstars.

During our first matchup, Elton jabbed to the right so effectively, I would have bet my D-League salary he was driving to the basket. I jumped back, creating a small window of opportunity for him, and that was all it took. He quickly rose and buried a three. *Holy Shit*, I thought as I made my way to the back of the line. The entire play took just two seconds. The next time we lined up, Elton jabbed again, but this time I was not so easily fooled. I kept my balance and put a hand directly in Elton's face. He pivoted to the left. I stayed right with him. He took one hard dribble while I remained glued to his hip. I was taught to do from a young age to watch other players hips. I noticed Elton was preparing to jump. I quickly exploded into the air with my hands as high as they could go, preparing to block the shot of an NBA All-Star. Elton, however, had remained on the ground as I flew past him. He waited just a millisecond, then pulled up for another jumper that swished through the net. Elton-2; Me-0. Warmups wrapped up, and I already felt defeated. We began to pair up into teams for five on five.

And then there was Reggie.

Now, I have played some strong people, and I have played some quick people, but I have never played anyone like him. No matter where I went, he was there. If I sprinted down the floor, he sprinted right next to me. If I made a post move, he did everything he could to stop me. I felt like I was playing in the NBA Finals. But it wasn't the NBA Finals; it was a meaningless scrimmage at a meaningless practice. Or at least that was the thought process I had at the time. To an NBA player, there never is a meaningless game. For me, it meant everything, and to him, it should have been perceived as just another practice. But not for Reggie. Being an NBA player means you bring everything you have every time you step on the court, and not just when you are fighting for a job. A lesson I learned first-hand that day. To be where Reggie was, I needed to out-work everyone, out-hustle everyone and out-rebound everyone every second of every day. Reggie did that, and that is why he had a contract, and I did not.

Unfortunately for me, this was the man standing between me and a roster spot for the 76ers. I refused to back down and occasionally was able to score on him. Whenever this happened, the rage in Reggie's eyes grew to a level I had only seen when I dropped a bowl of Lucky Charms on the kitchen floor, just seconds after my dad told me to stay at the table and not leave my seat.

I am fairly certain Reggie had a bet with the rest of the team that I would not score, or he would be buying steak dinners at Del Friscos. I remember everyone giving a loud "OHHHHHHHH NOOOOOO REGGGGGGG!" every time I made a shot.

Oh my god, guys, please don't piss him off any more than he already is. Instead of scanning the neighborhood for a parent to escape The Dudes, I scanned the court, only to find everyone encouraging him to eat my soul. I quickly remembered standing up to the bigger guy as a kid and knew at that moment no one was going to help me. It was up to me. I had to fight for my place on this team. Since most of you have never heard of me, you figured out the outcome of my tenure as a Philadelphia 76er. I can't help but think, my road to the NBA could have been a little easier had Reggie been caught in traffic that morning.

I walked out of the gym with a better understanding of hard work and about a dozen or so deep lacerations all over my arms and chest. I now have an even greater appreciation of the talent in the NBA. I am quick to correct anyone who claims an

NBA player *stinks*. Usually followed by "If he stinks, what do you think of me?" as I quickly walk away before they give me an unwanted answer.

My NBA career was short; in fact, it was so short, some people will say it did not exist. While my cup of espresso with the highest league in basketball did not end up how my dreams perceived it, I did walk away with a life lesson: No matter what you are doing, make sure you bring every ounce of energy to your craft every single day. If you don't, the Reggie Evans of the world will.

Part 2

International Career

Heading Abroad

I remember my last D-League game vividly. We were in Fort Worth, Texas, and had just lost in the semifinals. My D-League career was over. I wandered around downtown Fort Worth after the game with two things on my mind. First, how to avoid all the people chasing me down the street shouting "Dirk!" At the time, and I guess still now, I bear a slight resemblance to future NBA Hall of Famer Dirk Nowitzki because of my height, long hair, and probably not my basketball ability. My second thought was a sense of finality to my professional career. I had spent three years trying to make the NBA and was no closer than when I began. And worst of all, I had no money to show for it. I had given every ounce of my heart to the Roanoke Dazzle yet was still struggling to make a car payment.

I opened my T-Mobile Sidekick and began emailing Geoff, who was thousands of miles away in Mulhouse, France. I mentioned how pissed I was that this year was a waste. How I worked so hard to get to where I needed to be, only to deal with politics during my last year. I should have tried to push for another overseas job when I left Poland instead of returning to Roanoke. I sat on a bench outside a Texas coffee house at two o'clock in the morning spewing my emotional frustrations into a two-page email. A few minutes later, he responded with, "That sucks. Dad has to have surgery, isn't able to fly, and can't make his pre-booked trip. Come instead. -Geoff." Brevity was always my brother's thing, not wasting his voice, or in this case, his fingers on unnecessary dialogue.

A week later, I had packed up my life, waved goodbye to Roanoke, Virginia, and was back in South Jersey, not knowing what my next step would be. I seriously considered a new career. I was watching an episode of *The Wire* in my fetal semi-depressed state on the disgusting couch I bought off Craigslist when my phone, which had fallen into one of the many small crevices, began buzzing. I fished through the filth, grabbed my cell phone, and flipped it open.

It was my dad reiterating exactly what my brother had told me via email a week earlier. He had to get minor surgery, but the timing put a wrench into his perfectly planned vacation. He was now in need of a replacement, as the reservation was nonrefundable and would go to waste.

"Your brother has been in France for nine months and needs a boost in morale," he stated. "If you can use this trip, it would be a great experience."

I had just made it home myself, after being gone for seven months, and was not exactly jumping off my gross couch to leave again. I did not know how important that trip would be both for Geoff and me at the time. Being the spoiled asshole I was, I reluctantly accepted the free trip to Paris and Mulhouse. I re-packed my bags and headed to Europe for a week and a half.

I arrived in Mulhouse jet-lagged but excited to experience a foreign country without the obligation of having to perform on the basketball court. After a day of adjusting to my new environment, I sat with my brother in a cafe beside the Place de la Réunion, a large open square in downtown Mulhouse, and broke down my thoughts of early retirement from professional basketball. I could not fathom wasting more time and making less money. My brother had devoted a great deal of effort towards my career and couldn't spare the thought of me wasting it. Like Obi-Wan Kenobi trying to sway a young Anikan Skywalker from joining the dark side, he shared with me how talented he believed I had become and how I couldn't waste my proverbial force.

It was a hard sell as my brother had to go to practice, and I had the freedom to do whatever I wanted. Freedom to not exhaust my body with running and weight training and basketball workouts, a ritual I had been performing daily since high school. I could have a beer, eat what I wanted, go where I wanted, and do what I wanted without worrying about being out of shape.

My brother stood up to go to practice while dreams of day drinking in a French bar and eating crepes danced through my head. He turned back to me with a half-smile, "Why don't you come with me and get a run in? You can get a feel for the team and see if overseas basketball is as bad as you have made it out to be."

My face was a sinking ship. I had spent the last week and a half abusing my body with alcohol and cholesterol without even so much as a fast-paced walk. I had no interest in anything but a vacation. My ego, however, which had taken a hit this past season, peaked. I had spent the past seven months competing against NBA-level competition. I could handle a few Frenchies.

"Hold up," I yelled to him as he walked towards the arena. "Toss me your keys. I'll go grab my stuff." I had packed basketball gear instinctually without much thought, as every suitcase, I packed since my senior class trip to Disney World required it.

Despite the slight belly I developed during my two-week athletic hiatus, I was still a force to be reckoned with on the basketball court. I went through the rigors of a French Pro League B practice, much like Johnny and Cobra Kai dismantled Daniel Larusso in *The Karate Kid*. This delighted the American-born FC Mulhouse Basket coach, who was happy to have his team compete against a high-caliber player. And at this point, I was a high-caliber basketball player. It took an overseas professional basketball practice to truly realize how good I had become. Geoff and his infinite wisdom had struck again. I WAS way too talented to retire. While I was determined to enjoy the remainder of the trip, I knew the grind would continue when I got home. It had become unmistakably obvious I could make serious money playing this game, and I knew the D-League and France were to thank for that.

Flying home from Paris, after three remarkable days exploring the French capital by foot, I knew I would be going all-in on landing an overseas contract. My three-year relationship with the D-League was over. It was bittersweet. My comfort level with the town and the league itself was high, and moving on to a new environment would take some adjusting. But it was a step I was willing to take to gain financial success as a professional athlete.

Chapter 5

The Good, the Bad, and the Ugly...Suit

Ever since I was a child, I've had some odd attraction to medieval culture. I believe it began with *Star Wars* and the foam lightsaber I used to fend off my dog when she would try to eat food off my plate. As the years passed, a Wiffle Ball bat replaced the foam lightsaber, then a hockey stick, and after attending a Weapons Expo in Roanoke, a real sword. Correction, a collection of real swords, none of which were used directly on my dog; however, if a dragon ever flies into my bedroom, I'll be ready.

The obsession continued with the completely inappropriate movies I watched growing up. I had a sister who was six years my senior. I imagine my dad did not feel like getting several movies at Blockbuster, and being that we only had one TV, he would get a film that he and my sister would enjoy. The rest of us would watch *Goodfellas* or *Silence of the Lambs*, and they would deal with the trauma and nightmares later.

One evening, after being told to put *The Land Before Time* back on the shelf in favor of *Silver Bullet,* my dad decided to take advantage of Blockbuster's two-for-one deal and picked up a movie titled *Willow*. I remember sitting on the floor with a big chunk of Big-League Chew gum, watching a scantily clad Princess Sorsha, holding a knife up to Madmartigan's neck and thinking, *this is what love must be like*. I must have watched that movie fourteen times during the three-day rental. *Willow* had everything: swords and battles, magic and Warwick Davis, whom I idolized. Geoff always pretended to be the badass Val Kilmer, while I aspired to be the 3-foot 6-inch protagonist despite having a father who is 6-feet 7-inches tall and a mother who is 6-feet 2-inches. This combination would lead me to Sunday evenings thirty years later, watching *Game of Thrones*.

The show's appeal is more than just gratuitous nudity and violence that my male mind finds so enjoyable. It is the story, the unbridled success, and the notion that things can go drastically wrong on any given day, rocking the storyline and future forever. That is why this show is so popular. No one is safe from death and despair. That even the mightiest warriors or most powerful kings must one day face their doom. Plus, it has Tyrion Lannister, the best character in all of the stage and screen. I know I am 7-feet tall, and I get the irony of that, but Peter Dinklage legitimately rocks the shit out of every scene.

Which, in a roundabout fucking way, brings me to my point. No matter how positive a profession can be, we all must deal with the gruesome details that keep the story interesting. That even toughest and most experienced players will struggle. And that all players have felt said struggle. Some being spit on by opposing fans, or not being paid, or being released under shady circumstances, or hurting their knee and being sent home despite that team breaching contract and still owing hundreds of thousands of dollars. But this is what makes the storyline so interesting. People do not tune in for the good times. They want to see the bad and the ugly. And as a professional athlete, sometimes you need the rough patches to realize how good life can be in the right situation.

Sometimes what you think is an ideal situation turns problematic quickly, circa Poland 2004. I accepted a contract for $9,000 US per month to play in Włocławek, Poland. I flew to Poland crammed into a coach seat, next to a guy who looked like Clark from *The Office*. Shortly after takeoff, he became a drunken idiot. He spent most of the eight-hour flight telling me, in broken English, how he was a student at The University of Pennsylvania and was working on *some top secret shit*. He never revealed his mission, but he did spill red wine on my arm several times.

I should have taken this as an omen, but I hated flying and spent the eight hours thinking every bump was going to be the end of my life. Arriving safely on the ground set my mind at ease during the two-hour drive to Włocławek. That is until we pulled up to the graffiti-covered arena. The large concrete monstrosity served as my training facility for the next nine months. It wasn't a mural of the team or some sort of street art, but random illicit blue and black scribblings covering the wall to the player's entrance. I'm unsure why this stuck out in my mind or why it was all I could notice, but this was a professional basketball team offering more money than I had ever seen, and the building looked like an absolute shithole.

At that time, I assumed the internet was a giant collection of factual data and that it would never lie to me. I usually Asked Jeeves for information about the city I would be living in. The images never showed the dilapidation caused by war, neglect or random people being dicks. Instead, the internet focused on the beautiful European structures that lined the center of the city. The beautiful pieces of art I remembered from my search a few days before were replaced by the grey concrete building that stood before me.

The crazy thing about basketball is that no matter where you go, it remains the same. The rules are the same. The rims are the same. The court is the same. Everything within the lines of the wooden territory is familiar. Outside those lines, that is a different story.

This Polish gym was no different than the gyms I had spent countless hours in before that day. It had wood floors, a three-point line and an orange rim. I unpacked my shoes and joined my first practice just twenty minutes after I arrived in Włocławek.

Practicing right after a cross-continental flight is never pretty. Some people call it *getting the plane out of you.* I call it *trying not to poop myself after eating Polish KFC on the drive from the airport.* Regardless, that first practice was rough. My legs were not working, my shots weren't falling, and my lungs were exhausted. Luckily, my ass cheeks were making up for the muscle fatigue in other areas of my body, or it would have been an embarrassing first day.

I was scheduled to make a decent amount of money that year in exchange for my ability to hustle, rebound and score, while also being a good role model for the youngsters of Poland. Before I left, Geoff and few other overseas basketball veterans told me to check my bank account the day I was scheduled to be paid. Overseas front offices are notorious for playing games. Seeing that I had never had a job where a paycheck wasn't waiting for me on payday, I assumed the game they were referring to was UNO. However, a week in, I checked my account, and the promised money was still not there. Assuming this was just an oversight by my team or just a glitch in the newfangled internet, I did not go into panic mode. The next day I asked fellow import Albert Mourning if he received his money. Albert responded with an enthusiastic, "Fuck, no!"

At this point, I had been in Poland for two weeks and was holding my own in my first European pro basketball experience. Knowing that lack of pay usually meant a plane ticket home was imminent, I began to panic. I needed some verification that I was playing well enough to stay from someone familiar with this team. I spoke to my English-speaking teammate, Donatas Zavackas as we began practice by running around a grass field for some reason. Donatas told me to rest assured, they like to play money games, and I was playing well and should not fear my release. He told me I need to make sure they know I am not a pushover and demand my money.

Since I was not good at confrontation, I decided to stay the course and trust the ownership. A few days later, I rechecked my account, and still, there was only the paltry amount made during my two years in the D-League and the short stint I had working at Rita's Water Ice as a gelati barista in high school. I was officially panicked. I had traveled halfway across the world hoping to make my fortune, yet money was still being a little bitch. I immediately made an expensive international phone call to my agent to explain the situation. He, too, told me to stay the course. I obliged. Another day, another missed payment. Donatas' words began replaying over and over in my head. I had to do something. But what? I was twenty-five years old. Was I supposed to walk into the office of a team that has been around for decades demanding my money from a group of foreign men who could have made their fortune by feeding 6-feet 10-inch men like myself to the pigs?

I needed a pep talk! Unfortunately, my dad, who was prone to inspirational speeches, was 4,251 miles away. I remember standing in front of the mirror, repeatedly threatening my reflection, demanding money. I was pretty convincing. If I had any money to my name, I would have handed it over to the creep in the mirror. I was bustling with confidence when I walked into the practice facility the next day. I had even thought about some heartwarming stories I could use in case the whole aggressive approach did not work out.

I was ready. The next day I headed to claim what was rightfully mine. I popped into the locker room to quickly knock out some pushups so I would feel a little stronger. I was on my seventeenth pushup when our assistant walked in and told me and Albert, who also was still not paid, to meet the owner in the office. This was confusing. I was the aggressor here. I wanted to see them, not the other way around. They threw me off my game. I had to regroup. I was ten feet from the office, and I had lost my nerve. I stepped through the door of the smoky, dimly lit room and sat down across from the man who held my financial future in his hands.

Say something! I repeatedly screamed in my head. I had to be the one who makes the first move. It was the ultimate tic tac toe game, and I had to establish the center box and not be royally fucked. I started to speak, "I noti—"

I was quickly interrupted by our owner, who began speaking in a low voice, "Gentlemen, we need to release you two both."

I was stunned. I did not know what to say or do. He had completely taken me off my game. I think the only verbal speech I could muster was something like, "Ughhhh." He then thanked us for our time and walked out.

Where are you going, you little bitch? I said in my head. This was a nightmare. His exit was followed immediately by the entrance of a small woman carrying a small bag. She pulled out a large stack of $100 bills and began counting out $3,000 each—a small percentage of my monthly salary. I was expected to make far more than that each month, but I was not exactly in a position of power at the moment. "Excuse me, Ma'am," I asked. "What is happening? Where is the rest of the money? Why are we being released?" She glanced up at me with a look of *I do not make the decisions, nor do I speak English,* and walked out.

Albert and I sat in stunned silence for a minute or two before our driver walked in and ushered us to the car. I spoke to my agent, who tried to tell me to stay put while he found another team who wanted to pick me up. I was already in Europe, which made it an easier sell since an international ticket did not need to be purchased. This whole experience had momentarily soured me on playing outside of America. I had spoken to my friend Seth Doliboa, who was in Roanoke waiting for the season to begin, and decided I wanted to give this NBA thing one more chance.

My agent reluctantly agreed, and I was flown home after just a few short weeks in Poland. I would later learn the same situation occurred multiple times that season. Imports were shipped in and out that year like Amazon packages. This was my first trip abroad as a professional basketball player, and it screwed up my whole mindset towards European basketball.

There was some good news in this situation. I was in better shape and $3,000 richer than I was a month before. I had arrived home right before my family was scheduled to make an appearance for the Philadelphia Phillies. My Grandfather, Paul "The Pope" Owens, was the former GM and Manager of the Phillies during their magical 1980 Championship run. Every year we present an award in his name.

At this point, I was still scheduled to make chump change in the D-League and my dreams of a lifted pickup truck with enormous chrome rims were fading. I needed a pick-me-up; something that would show off the glamorous career I had chosen for myself.

My brother was off in France playing for LNB Pro B team Mulhouse, which made me the primary presenter of the Phillies outstanding award. Unfortunately, my wardrobe was that of a guy who made a total of $24,000 two years out of college. The only suit I owned was the same one I wore to numerous high school dances where I would try, often unsuccessfully, to end up naked with a member of the opposite sex. I needed an upgrade, something worthy of a man with $3,000 in crisp American currency in his pocket.

Buying a suit is not easy for a man of my impressive physique. I can't run into the Banana Republic and grab something off the rack, as it would fit much like the suit Pee Wee Herman wore while riding cross country with Large Marge. I mentioned my situation to former NBA veteran and current Philadelphia 76er analyst Mark Jackson, with whom I had been spending my summer mornings training alongside. He told me about a place called Torre Big and Tall located in South Philadelphia. They specialized in vertically gifted people like me. At the time, I had no idea what was stylish, as the late '90s and early '00s were a confusing time for fashion. I did know one thing...no one wore a suit better than the cast of *The Sopranos*. The thought of owning a pinstripe suit was an exciting prospect for me. Beaming with confidence, I entered Torre Big and Tall.

Sardined into this small shop were thousands of multi-colored suits of all shapes and sizes, most leaning towards the *big* aspect of *Big and Tall*. Pictures of famous athletes like Wilt Chamberlain, Charles Barkley, and every offensive and defensive lineman in Philadelphia Eagles history adorned the walls. A small gentleman walked up to me and asked what I was shopping for. I told him about the suit, the budget and the pinstripes. He sat me down on their couch and worked to find me the perfect outfit. I'm going to reiterate this: I was very naive about what a suit should look and fit like and that no one should spend over $500 on one.

A few minutes later, he returned, holding in his hands the worst decision I ever made. The suit he held up was brown with alternating blue and orange pinstripes. Me being a complete freaking idiot, was unsure but enamored with the fabric. Any reservations I had were quickly rectified by the savvy salesman who told me this was very fashionable and that he just sold the same suit to Donovan McNabb a few weeks ago. At that time, he was the star quarterback for the Eagles and, in my mind, exemplified the wealthy, well-to-do look I was going for. I tried the suit on, which should have been my second clue. It was just brown fabric draping off my body like a curtain.

"We will tailor it to your body," the salesman assured me.

I reluctantly agreed. Being that he already unloaded the Sesame Street Snuffleupagus suit on my dumbass, he figured he would go for the trifecta by showing me two shirts. One shirt appeared to be an almost teal blue, and the other shirt a mustard yellow at only $60 each. The matching tie, resembling the color of vomit, was thrown in as well for an additional $45—my total bill for this complete disaster: $1,012.36.

I took out my collection of crisp $100 dollar bills and began counting them on the counter. For the first time in my life, I was a big timer. I had a hideously gross suit, a small stack of hundreds, and I was going to wow them at the presentation. A few days later, after I had taken some time away from the situation, I went to pick up the suit. Upon trying it on, I discovered that I looked like a kid wearing his dad's clothes. It was very boxy, think every player in the 2003 NBA Draft. The jacket was long, nearly down to my knees. The pinstripes were weird, and the overwhelming brownness of the suit was intoxicating to my eyes. I had to do something. I was set to go in front of a crowd of people in a few days, and I would look like a pinstriped pimp. I marched back into Torre's and asked if my suit could be altered, returned or placed into an incinerator. The salesman who saw me as nothing more than a giant dollar sign not only convinced me that the suit was stylish and a perfect fit, but somehow also convinced me that I needed a new pair of shoes for one-hundred and twenty dollars. Money was officially burning a hole in my pocket.

I wore the suit three days later for the first and last time while enduring insults from my family members and anyone in attendance at the Phillies game that evening. To recap, I had spent $1,132.36, and all I had to show were a few pictures of me looking ridiculous next to Phillies star Ryan Howard. The suit made its way to the back of my closet and eventually Goodwill, where my only hope was that it made its way into the hands of someone who could wear it to Dave Chapelle's *Player Haters Ball*.

That year I learned a lot about trust; about what to look for when trusting people. Whether it is an agent, the owner of a team, or a shady salesperson trying to sell you a shitty suit, what may look great on paper, could have a far different outcome. Trust is a funny thing in overseas professional basketball, especially when contracts are not guaranteed. You are performing on a month-to-month basis. If there is an injury or a slump, or the management simply realizes they won't be able to stay out of the red, the team will void the contract, and the only compensation received is a one-way ticket home. It is a shitty broken system, but if you want a shot at a professional career, you need to trust the system, even if it will burn you in the end.

Chapter 6

The Land Down Under

Having zero responsibilities for an extended period is one aspect of life we don't appreciate as a child. Instead, as a twelve-year-old, I would get bored and ask my parents for a snack or to take me somewhere because a day with nothing to do or no one to play with was unbearable.

Even in my twenties, I didn't have an appreciation for time. While I was not so much a kid, my friends still called me Peter Pan because I got paid to play a game and admittedly had not yet reached that mental maturity I currently possess. Back then, I was my own boss and had to manage my time well enough to continue excelling on the basketball court, while the rest of my time was left for whatever shenanigans I felt like engaging. This is why I did not appreciate the day-long chance to sit and binge-watch whatever show I wished in a comfortable emergency exit row during the three-plane, cross-continent-cross-ocean trip to Cairns, Australia. Instead, because I am a complete psychotic idiot, I spent those twenty-seven hours gripping the seat, mentally willing the plane to not share the same fate as the passengers from the television show *Lost*.

This long trip was a necessary evil, escorting me safely to paradise where I would be joining the Cairns Taipans of the NBL (Australian National Basketball League). Cairns truly was paradise. It is the American equivalent to Miami, but without all the neon and coke, at least that was my perception. The weather is tropical, the people are friendly, and the women are beautiful. I lived in a second-floor resort condo, with one balcony overlooking a golf course and the other the Playboyesque pool and grotto. I had a brand-new car with our logos plastered all over which I learned to drive on the opposite side of the road, nearly killing multiple pedestrians, several marsupials, and, more importantly, myself. My teammates were an incredible group who immediately took me in and made me feel like I had been part of the team my whole life. The organization paid me well and gave me every opportunity to explore their beautiful land, which is how I ended up on a floating pontoon structure in the middle of the Pacific Ocean, trying to sardine myself into a tight, bright blue wetsuit.

"Mate, it will be tight as, but try this wettie. It's the biggest we got," one of the crew members of the tour stated.

I held the blue wetsuit up next to my enormous body, noticing the large size discrepancy. *There is no way all of me is fitting into this tiny thing.* I looked around the boat while the rest of the smurfs prepared for their snorkeling excursion on the Great Barrier Reef, donning their blue wetsuit.

"Do I really need this?" I asked our Australian guide, naively holding up the stretchy piece of fabric. "I don't mind the cold."

"Mate, if ya jump in there with just ya togs on, the stingers are gonna fully rip ya up."

Stingers are what the Aussies called box jellyfish, one of the many things capable of killing me, lurking beneath the surface of the crystal-clear water. I had taken a catamaran thirty miles off the coast of Cairns, Australia, into the middle of the ocean. It was my first break since I had arrived in paradise, and the team had arranged a snorkeling trip.

"So what can kill me in here?" I sarcastically asked my tour guide. While I was aware, this was a loaded question, the realization of how loaded the question was became apparent during his answer.

"Most dangerous are the stingas (box jellyfish), but watch for poisonous ocky (blue-ringed octopus) and sea snakes (faint-banded sea snake). Basically, don't touch anything that is movin down there, especially the coral (that shit is poisonous too). The tiga shawk (tiger shark) doesn't come around till lata in the arvo (afternoon), and we will be back to shore by that time. The salties (saltwater crocodiles) stay close to land, so if you see a large shadow, it's probably yaself, Mate."

"So, what now Scott, I'm supposed to just jump in the ocean?" I asked in a higher voice than usual due to the blue pressure on my testicles. Scott was my Australian teammate and personal guide to the dangers of Australia. He had played his college basketball in the States, where he met his American wife, Erica, who had become close friends with my then fiancé Sara. Scott and Erica would frequent our condo for dinners or drinks, or occasionally a personal *Crocodile Hunter* experience.

There are a few things you should know about Australians just in case you have not had the pleasure yet. First, Aussies are the nicest people on the planet. I honestly did not meet one single dickhead in Australia unless they were another nationality. I had people sacrificing their time or offering a helping hand daily. One guy even offered me a set of golf clubs if I ever felt like playing a round, despite him being almost a foot shorter than me. They are, without a doubt, the friendliest of all humans.

The second thing you need to know about Australians is while they are remarkably nice, they are also crazy. Like, absolutely freaking crazy. They have very little fear of the things that keep me and you up at night. The most common fears amongst ordinary people are public speaking, insects and drowning. These three things don't affect the average outgoing Aussie. I once saw a maintenance man at the resort pick up a huntsman spider and throw it across the small creek that ran along the property's perimeter. The spider was the size of his hand, and he tossed it aside like a piece of trash.

The final thing you need to know about Australians is that they also possess a unique toughness. You mouth off to them, and they will knock you out, then help you up. The same occurs on the basketball court. Guys would draw a hard foul, turn around and say something along the lines of, "You wanna have a go ya cunt?"

The other guy would fire right back, "Ga head ya deackhead (dickhead)." They would throw punches, storm off, and then be laughing and drinking a beer together twenty minutes later. Again tough, but friendly.

Australians use their fists to settle disputes. Gun violence is not a thing down under, as they can just pick up one of the multiple poisonous things surrounding them at all times and throw it at someone for the same effect. That is why when you see someone messing with dangerous animals, chances are they are Australian. Something I saw first-hand when Scotty Cook would show up some evenings with some sort of frog, or lizard, or one time, a two-foot-long stick insect which I allowed to crawl on my neck so I wouldn't appear terrified. I screamed on the inside.

"Jump as far out as ya can so ya don't have to swim through the deep stuff," Scott yelled as he floated comfortably in the ocean like it was a pool. The deep stuff was the middle of the ocean, fifty meters from the coral reef we would be exploring. Michael Phelps swims that distance in about twenty-one seconds. This meant that, although I am a strong swimmer, there were about thirty seconds, give or take, of me dangling at the surface of the ocean while a shark lined me up to be ambushed like the *Air Jaws* programs I had watched during Shark Week every year since I was twelve.

I looked out to the vast water surrounding me, knowing exactly how far I was from medical attention. I closed my eyes, told myself *fuck it*, and jumped into the abyss containing 90% of my fears. My feet splashed into the water. Panic began to set in. I began floundering on the surface, much like a wounded animal. *Jesus Christ Kevin, calm down! This is exactly what the sharks want.*

"Breathe, Mate," Scotty shouted at me as he glided on the surface with little concern. I took a deep breath and began slowing the spastic thrashing down. I looked up to the sky and trusted that whatever was lurking below cared little about me. My fins eventually hit the hard surface of the shallow reef below me. I had done it. I had embraced my fear and lept into a different world. It was both terrifying and liberating. My mind began to relax and focus on the beauty that surrounded me.

Since my career began, I lived in Poland, Virginia, or my childhood bedroom for three years and experienced very little. But here I was, in one of the Natural Wonders of the World, watching the cast of *Finding Nemo* swim around me. It was a surreal moment when the realization of how incredibly blessed I had become set in. I was exploring the Great Barrier Reef on break from playing professional basketball for a team that was paying me shit tons of money.

I had a bit of a swagger before, which tends to happen after playing high-level basketball long enough. I wouldn't say I was a cocky asshole, but I was way better than the skinny unconfident kid I used to be. Floating in this salty sea, I started reflecting while the back of my brain kept a close eye out for sharks. Shitty basketball players don't end up in situations like this. Only extremely talented ones make it this far. I was not here as a charity case or because I was someone's brother. I was here because I earned it. My confidence grew like the colorful coral on this underwater ecosystem.

In all my years, I had never been the superstar. In my senior year of high school and throughout college, I was considered the *guy*, meaning many teams game planned against me, but personally, I never perceived myself as the best player on the court. I was taught the importance of team basketball from an early age and considered shooting too much as a negative.

After my excursion exploring the reefs of Northern Queensland, my mindset began to shift. I could remain a team player, but as an import, I needed to be more aggressive on the offensive end. Thousands of Australians could be team players; I needed to be something more, a point my Taipan coaches had been stressing for several weeks. While I always prided myself on being the best rebounder, I now needed to add scoring to my resume if I were to be successful overseas.

I began studying the nuances of the offense—a slip of a screen here, a quick seal on a post-up there. I identified the defensive weaknesses and attempted to put myself in ideal scoring positions. I had always thought the way to score was by rebounding. I never approached the game with a scorer's mindset, thinking that my points needed to come off rebounds or designed post-ups. My scoring average began to rise as I focused more on the offensive portion of the game. I was capable of this but needed to overcome the mental barriers my mind had for some reason created sort of like riding my bike for the first time, an experience both exhilarating and traumatic. I had been riding with training wheels for some time before my parents forcefully eliminated the mental barriers by pushing me down the street at high speed. While my feeble hands tried to stabilize the wobbly handlebars, I drifted to the grass before losing control and crashing into a parked car.

I needed to do a similar exercise on the basketball court. I needed to break through my lack of confidence which prevented me from being a selfish player. The only way to do that was by shooting the ball every opportunity I could. The elimination of my basketball mental blocks had a more positive result than me slamming face-first into a Buick. I averaged double figures and was one of the top rebounders in the league. I even earned a spot on the World All-Star Team, the first All-Star nomination of my professional career. I joined the top players in the league in front of a packed crowd, many of whom mocked me about my high socks.

Australia had incredibly passionate fans. Playing in the NBL was a lot like playing in the NBA. The crowd was large and loud, and they were not lighting shit on fire and throwing it at you, like other experiences in my career. The fans in Cairns, particularly, supported me from the start through all the ups and downs. They were kind and very intelligent. They knew the game well and understood the hard work we put in. They were also very excited to meet us when we did come across them in the community. It was a unique experience, and for the first time in my life, I felt like a celebrity.

I had moments of importance in college when we made the NCAA Tournament for the first time, and the campus embraced us...some more than others. Or when I came home to my local bar after my first few years of professional basketball and was treated to free food and drinks. But nothing compared to this.

This brings me to the next thing you need to know about Australians. They know how to party. Like really love to party! If I were to name every wild teammate I played with, Australians would make up most of the list. They are always the life of the party, making every social encounter in Australia wildly entertaining, which brings me to Coffs Harbour, Australia, and my first night out with the team.

We were on the first road trip of our young season, and so far, I had been fairly isolated from the fans. I mean, aside from my buddy Alan Aldous, a young fan who would show up on my doorstep and occasionally ask for rides. As I previously mentioned, Australian basketball has more of an NBA atmosphere. In Australia, there were short quick interactions in and out of the tunnel. It was not as personal as Roanoke, Virginia, where we would have personal relationships with our fans. In Cairns, the large Convention Center sold out regularly, and after-parties with only the team's ownership were held in the local casino. So far, I had not had a taste of regular Aussie nightlife. This night would be my first.

We were playing in Coffs Harbour, Australia, the host of the NBL's Preseason Blitz. The Blitz brought all twelve teams to one location for a group tournament. I had a breakout game before we eventually lost in the playoff stage. After our final day playing, we decided to head out to a local hot spot for some Australian shenanigans instead of going back to the hotel. One of the many cool things about the NBL was how inclusive the teams were. The entire team headed out that night as a pack. As we arrived, players from many other teams greeted us. They, too, were equally excited about Coffs Harbour nightlife.

Back then, I was not the sharp dresser I am today. This is before I discovered Pinterest and noticed how normal people should be dressing, and years before American Eagle made tall clothes, allowing me to look like a normal human and not a struggling Seattle rockstar. My clothes were baggy and stupid, and I looked out of place amongst my well-dressed teammates. Later that year, at the All-Star Game, I would ask legendary Australian center Paul Rodgers where he got his jeans. He probably thought I was such a tool, but that next summer, I finally looked liked part of the gang.

The club was rocking. We had a connection with the bar owner and drank for free. Bar owners love when local celebrities drink in their establishment because it brings every smoke show Australian hottie to the club, bringing the geeks who think they have a shot. It is a win-win for everyone, besides the lonely, thirsty dudes who will end up eating french fries at 3 am, talking about how a hot girl accidentally touched their leg.

Oh, and another thing you need to know about Australians, they drink a lot. And they do not get sick, ever. I would watch them crawl into a cab so incoherently inebriated, I swore they would be dead the next morning, only to arrive hungover as shit to lifting practice and they'd be all happy like, "How ya goin, KO? Did ya chunder last night, Mate?" I would spend the session trying not to vomit while they threw weights around like we didn't do shots till four o'clock in the morning the night before.

I've never been to the Playboy Mansion, and now since the passing of Hugh Heffner, probably never will, but this bar in Coffs Harbor was as close as I'll ever get. Aussie girls are hot, and I think one third of them were in attendance. There were beautiful women everywhere you looked, and they were actually talking to me. This was a newer feeling, considering I was what my Mom referred to as a late bloomer. Having models smiling and talking to me was a new experience. At that time in my life, I was engaged and about to be married. Smiling and talking was as exciting as my night was going to get. But I was not the only piece of meat on display that evening.

The girls played an extremely competitive game of *Who Can Be Impregnated by a Taipan*. In Australia, if you have a child, you hit the financial lottery. Five thousand dollars is awarded to you by the Australian Government. Plus, the prospect of a famous rich baby daddy made the stakes of this game very high. Most of my teammates had wives or serious girlfriends, so they spent the evening in a similar situation as me. However, the ones who were single had their pick of any of the contestants in this X-Rated game. I recall one teammate making out with one girl by the bathroom, and just a few minutes later, a different girl at the bar. I couldn't even order a drink that quickly.

The night escalated, as did the friskiness of the female population. We had an early flight the next morning and had begun coming up with an exit plan. As hard as it was to depart a beach-side bar filled with beautiful women, the temptation was growing too strong. The bartender had called us a cab to take us safely back to the hotel. We started to assemble our crew and head for the exit. That was until an unthinkable event occurred. The women followed us. Not all the women, but around 15-20, or one for each player and two for others. (Winkey Face Emoji)

We spilled out in front of the club, waiting for the cab. The women surrounded us. Some were asking where we were staying. Others asked if there was room in the cab for them and eighteen of their friends. The two vans slowly pulled up. We began piling into the vehicles. Some of the more bold ladies attempted to jump in. A different set of women who had been setting up their own thirst traps all night began pulling the one set away and replacing themselves in our van. I was ten years old again watching *G.L.O.W* and wondering what was happening in *my* down under. *When did we become the Beatles?* The girls were pulled out by a bouncer while trying to grab hold of one of our young player's hands. I hopped out of the cab to survey the situation.

Several of my teammates were still making their way through the chaotic crowd. A few more had created a quasi-barricade to stop the adoring women from reaching the cab. The remaining teammates were sliding under the arms of the human barricade. One beautiful blonde slipped underneath, grabbed hold of one of the players, pulled his head down, and kissed him so passionately. I could have sworn I was watching a scene from *The Notebook*. We pulled him away from the clutches of the evil temptress and told the driver to get us out of there. The horny group continued banging on the windows as the cab pulled away from the club and onto the highway, and alas, we were safe, safe from the beautiful women trying to kiss us.

Interactions like this were not uncommon in Australia, where the women were beautiful, and in my case, blind. Unfortunately, I would not be known as the wild celebrity party boy on the Aussie circuit. Instead, I was occasionally called Big Kev, a reference to an excitable overweight cleaning supplies salesman, known for his catchphrase, "I'm Excited!"

Opposing fans used to yell that at me often. "HEY BIG KEV," they would scream. "ARE YOU EXCITED?" I would shake my head and give them a thumbs-up despite having a little clue what the fuck they were talking about.

What I would actually be known for in Australia was not the most flattering. During the year, my temper would fluctuate between *This is fucking awesome* to *How is that a foul* quickly. This is why I had a somewhat tumultuous relationship with referees, fans and opposing players that year. While my interactions were not always explosive, when they were, they were spectacular.

We had just advanced to the quarterfinal, where we would take a six-hour cross-continent trip to Challenge Arena, home of the Perth Wildcats with the title of the most difficult arena to play in Australia. We won our first playoff game in franchise history a few days earlier. A game where I, according to Paul Kennedy, FIBA correspondent, in Australia, "was *the star*, claiming the ground under the ring at each end and continually finishing off the good work of teammates." A quote that was without a doubt my favorite backhanded compliment I ever received. Opposing fans who once laughed at my high socks now feared me. We came into Perth as underdogs. Perth had finished towards the top of the table that year. Now I have no proof besides the tape of the game; however, I firmly believe someone did not want us to leave Perth with a victory.

I never saw a more poorly officiated game. For nine minutes, I was roughly guarded by an assortment of Perth players, to the point where after the game, I did not know whether to take a shower or a morning-after pill. Despite the physical play that was allowed on me, I was called for fouls they would not enforce in a third grade girl's game. I played a total of nine minutes that game and fouled out.

Now I am not an idiot. I knew how to play this game. In fact, I knew how to play this game well enough to be in this situation. This was the quarterfinals, and in an enormous match like this, I was going to use my head and not commit dumb fouls. But something that day told me no matter what I did, I would be watching the game from the sidelines.

I felt like Brett Hart during the infamous Montreal Screwjob where Vince McMahon, unbeknownst to Hart, changed the predetermined outcome of the title match in 1997's Survivor Series. Hart, who was supposed to retain his title prior to leaving WWE for WCW, was part of an elaborate ruse where The Heartbreak Kid, Shawn Michaels, locked Hart into his own signature move, the Sharpshooter. The ref called for a tap-out despite no tapping out occurring. Hart, irate at the screwjob, lost his mind, destroying equipment and punching Vince McMahon in the face.

I, like Hart, have an animosity that I hold deep in my soul for those referees that day. Every game I played as a professional basketball player influenced future jobs. This was not just about the team that night, as we ended up winning the game and moving on to the semifinals. But selfishly, had I played a dominant game in Perth, I could have played in Australia for longer than a year. Who knows what would have happened had the *Perth Screwjob* not taken place.

I wish that I could say that was the end of the story; however, the most embarrassing part has yet to unfold.

I am referring to what my friends call the *towel incident*, an incident that is still part of Australian lore. After *apparently* committing my final foul, I was in a blind rage. As I walked towards the bench, another player tossed me a towel to wipe off the nine minutes of sweat I had sporadically accumulated that night. I sat down at the end of the bench, ignoring the water being offered to me by our trainer, and bit down on the towel. My mind was in a particularly fragile state as I yanked down on the towel while maintaining the deathlock I still held with my teeth. The fabric of the towel had no chance against the monstrous three-way tug. It tore to shreds with remnants of towel ending up in my hands, while a large piece dangled out of my mouth like a piece of flesh being consumed by a large predator. I spit out a chunk of fabric, threw the remaining pieces of the towel under my chair, and went back to quietly sulking.

This whole situation, while primitive and a bit extreme, was my initial reaction. I figured since the game was still being played, no one noticed. One less towel, my teeth still functioning, everything would be fine. Unfortunately, the camera, which had followed my journey to the bench, stayed locked on me during my little temper tantrum. And that camera was transmitting a signal to a nationally televised audience, or pretty much the entire country of Australia.

Back in Cairns, the entire town had gathered at the famous Reef Hotel and Casino to watch the live broadcast on a jumbo screen. Sara had made her way to the casino to watch with the rest of the fans. When the infamous towel incident occurred, she became mortified. Not just because I had fouled out, but because everyone watching me rip the towel apart slowly turned towards her.

I had no idea this incident was being televised nationally until I picked up the phone after the game and Sara asked, "Should I make a dentist appointment?"

"I know, I got elbowed twice in my mouth and the refs didn't call shit!"

"That is not why I ask." Sara described how the camera stayed on me through my final foul, my walk to the bench, and my subsequent hissy fit. She described how everyone turned to her in horror after witnessing my towel murder. The next day highlights of our victory were all over the national news, complete with my towel tear. It was embarrassing and humiliating and also kind of cool. I have not tried towel ripping recreationally, but despite being a rage monster at the time, I don't think it requires too much force to rip a thin piece of cloth. The people of Australia, however, were under the illusion that I was some sort of lunatic. A title I relished for the last month of my Australian tenure.

While that *was* how I was remembered in Australia, in my mind, I held other distinctions. I had bounced back from the bench player role I held during my last D-League season and played better than I ever had. I held a koala bear, a python, a kangaroo, and various large insects. I swam in the middle of the ocean with multiple predators and stood on a rickety wooden bridge above 20-foot-long crocodiles. I explored a rainforest, a natural reef, and the Australian outback in the same week. There were lifelong friendships and lots of fans who made fun of my high socks. I was mentored by four legends of Australian basketball, who also happened to be my teammates, Robert Rose, Darnel Mee, Martin Cattalini and Anthony Stewart. Australia was where I fell in love with basketball. I had friend-zoned the game for a long time, knowing it was providing for me, but never fully embraced it.

In this exotic paradise, I fell in love with the game. I fell in love with the practice. I fell in love with the grind. And I fell in love with scoring. I had finally embraced the game that had given me so much. It would, unfortunately, be a short-lived relationship, as my newfound love for the game of basketball took me away from the land down under and into an awaiting nightmare.

Chapter 7

도대체 뭐야? (WTF?)

I am not a fan of Las Vegas. It never appealed to me. The large crowds, bright lights and loud noises are not really my thing. However, I do like to gamble, not exactly gambling in the traditional sense of the word, but more taking risks. It was never an easy philosophy to grasp. I was terrified each time I took a huge leap of faith but knew that I would live with regret if I never tried. From a young age, I was taught not to live with regret, to never pass on an opportunity presented to me because I was scared. On my wedding day, I danced with my mother to the Lee Ann Womack song, *I Hope You Dance*. The lyrics echoed the lesson I was taught all my life: take a chance! It is why I agreed to go to the Gambling Capital of the World to audition for an opportunity to make big money playing basketball in South Korea.

I had just completed my dream season in Australia and was looking for a new opportunity after the Taipans did not renew my contract. My heart broke knowing that I would not be one of the many American basketball players that went to Australia and never returned. I was disappointed but knew playing in South Korea was a chance to make big money.

The Korean camp had a similar setup to an NBA combine. But the NBA scouts were replaced by a group of men smoking cigarettes. There were coaches spread throughout, doctors checking joints, trainers measuring athletic abilities, and plenty of glitz and glamour from a league that pays six-figure salaries to twenty potential candidates. I had checked into the Monte Carlo just a few hours earlier before I hopped in the shuttle that took me to orientation. Again, I was a small fish in a big pond. I was coming off a successful year in Australia, but still, at twenty-seven years old, I had yet again to prove myself to a new set of admirers.

Playing professional basketball is a lot like speed dating. Every year you rotate around the room where you need to impress a brand-new team. You may be a great match to a potential suitor but are limited to these short observations of your abilities. It is impossible to tell the overall analytical composition of a basketball player after just a few days of drills and scrimmages, as it is unlikely to think you could fall madly in love with your soulmate in just a five-minute conversation.

The bright lights of Vegas paled in comparison to the pomp and circumstance of the Korean Basketball League orientation. The hotel ballroom was engulfed with logos adorning every wall, seat and fixture. An empty podium sat in the middle of a large stage. As close to 700 players filed into the conference room and sat down. After five minutes of awkward silence, a small man walked out to the podium and welcomed us. He introduced himself as a lawyer for the league and went over the shit-you-are-not-allowed-to-do list, which included drugs, alcohol, and being even a second late to anything from now until you are back in America after the season—that is if you are one of the twenty players selected in the draft at the conclusion of the weekend.

We signed page after page of *important* documents highlighting all the obligations we would be fulfilling if we were lucky enough to play in Korea. Interestingly enough, the contract did state if we were injured and projected to be out for an extended period, the team was REQUIRED to pay the rest of our salary.

The legality ended, and we were given the logistics of the camp. Basically, don't be lazy, don't be late and be readily available at all times. Ten groups sat courtside over the next two days behind their team logos while we did our best to impress enough to be one of the names called during the draft on the final evening. I was playing the best basketball of my life at the time and felt pretty confident in how I had performed that weekend. I had also recently unlocked athleticism I never knew existed, much like how you would upgrade a character in NBA 2K once you had stockpiled enough VC.

I was introduced to weight training in middle school when my dad added Geoff and me to his gym membership to bulk up our feeble frames. I spent most of my time there incorrectly using the machines and sitting in the sauna in my tighty whities. My next experience with lifting came in high school when we would bench press once a week. Knowledge of weight training was limited back then, so my gains were limited. By senior year I was maxing out with one to two reps of ninety-five pounds, a weight most children and the elderly could handle. I blamed it on my long arms and the large distance the weight needed to travel; however, the real reason being, I was weak as shit.

I began regularly lifting in college, but mainly to put on weight. Monmouth University was a small Division One university and therefore did not have the same financial prowess as a Duke or a UNC. Therefore Monmouth only had two strength coaches in the entire athletic department. These two coaches had to develop and monitor every Monmouth athlete's physical development throughout the year, an impossible task for such a small staff. Because of these circumstances, and the pre-social media world, where posting a ripped selfie with my shirt off was not yet a thing, my gains were limited. By the time I became a professional basketball player, I was yet to realize the full capabilities of the magnificent body given to me by God, Jesus, Allah, Buddha, evolution, or whatever denomination is the least offensive.

After each season, I would return home and reevaluate the weakest aspects of my game. My biggest weakness before this camp began was a lack of proper athleticism. In the D-League, I bulked up by lifting heavy weights. My bread and butter were rebounding and toughness, and I needed muscles to perform those tasks. I had knowledgeable coaches who worked one on one with me. I gained a great deal of muscle mass, helping me battle the monstrous opponents I would be facing in the D-League. When I arrived in Australia the following year, I was a step slower. I had spent so much time trying to gain mass that I had lost the quickness that separated me from the big goon football players I used to abuse in high school.

I watched a video on a new phenomenon sweeping the fitness nation called Crossfit. It consisted of explosive lifting combined with compound exercises. I spent my remaining summer days Crossfitting. Somewhat because of basketball and somewhat because it had drastically improved my jumping ability, something the strength shoes I wore and worked out in high school while enduring the ridicule of my neighbors never did. By the end of the summer, I was capable of the magic I remembered watching on Dazzling Dunks and Basketball Bloopers, another VHS I nearly wore out from constant viewing. At the camp I was attending in Vegas, this influx of athleticism made me the bell of the Korean ball, or so I thought.

Several Korean agents approached me, giving me the usual ass-kissing every basketball player has heard at one time or another. One, in particular, spoke to me over and over about how three teams were going to draft me. He had me convinced I would be picked that evening and not standing in the back of the conference room dumbfounded seconds away from kicking over an ice sculpture. Unfortunately, the worst-case scenario I had conjured up in my head would become a reality.

The draft was held at seven o'clock at night, a full eight hours after the championship game closing out the Korean camp. Because I was cheap and because I was not too fond of Vegas, staying another night in the expensive Monte Carlo was not an option unless someone handed me a large bag of cash that evening. My flight home was scheduled to leave at nine twenty-five that evening, and changing the flight would have added to my growing list of expenses on this trip. I sat and watched as player-after-player heard their names called, strolled up to the podium, were given a hat, a jersey, and the fruition of their dreams. Six hundred and sixty-one athletes had descended on Vegas that weekend with money signs in their eyes. I had outplayed most of them or at least 642 of them. If I were not at my best and was not told random lies by random people, I would have felt the decision to not draft me was justified. But that was not the case. I had gone to Vegas with big dreams, and like so many before me, I was going home empty-handed.

I always tried to keep my emotions in check. I was occasionally prone to angry outbursts growing up, but they were always justified. Most of the time, because a sibling gave me the younger brother treatment, I needed to defend myself. And sometimes, because I could not beat Ryu in *Street Fighter II* despite having his power down to a mere millimeter, something the posters covering the many holes I punched in the walls of my bedroom could attest for. But this was different. I could not cover up evidence of my anger with a Sports Illustrated cover. I WAS PISSED!

It was a different level of rejection than I was used to. It wasn't leaning in to kiss a girl and she puts her hand over her mouth, although that is pretty fucking awful. I had done everything in my power to earn a job, a job that had $200,000 riding on it. My mind began racing. *What could I have done differently? Could I have done more?* And for the first time in my life, I didn't second guess myself. I had done EXACTLY what I needed to do to earn that spot, which pissed me off even more. As the scouts called the last name, I aggressively grabbed my suitcase, muttered "Fuck this place," under my breath, and stormed out of the room, nearly kicking over the ice sculpture that inexplicably decorated the back table on my way out.

I hustled through the maze that was the inner workings of the Monte Carlo Resort, looking for the familiar red EXIT sign that would get me out of this miserable city. I managed to hail a taxi. The second the door closed, I lost my mind. The mortified driver, most likely thinking he had picked up someone with Tourette's Syndrome, drove as quickly as he possibly could to McCarran Airport for fear that I would rip his car apart like The Incredible Hulk. I still tune in to HBO's *Taxicab Confessions* to see if they caught my outburst and sandwiched it in between a drag queen and a threesome.

Sara, who had accompanied me on this trip, understood my frustration. She had heard all the conversations, watched all the games, and viewed all the bureaucratic bullshit that had us rushing to the airport with minimum time before our flight. She tried to calm me down for fear we would be banned from flying as my rage grew more apparent to any bystander within a twelve-mile radius. With just seconds to spare, I was on a plane away from Las Vegas, unemployed, and with no intent on ever associating with the KBL or Vegas, for that matter, ever again.

Believing that Korea was no longer an option, I focused my attention on finding a job for the following year. Two weeks and one wedding later, I was driving through Ocean City, NJ, when my phone rang. My agent, Mike Siegel, called. Not an unexpected phone call during late August, as most teams scramble to find players, and my name was put in for several jobs. I had spoken to him upon returning home from Vegas, venting my frustrations with the KBL tryout. Mike, knowing how well I had played, shared these frustrations. Which is why I was so surprised when I answered the phone to hear him say, "You still want to go to Korea?"

Mike explained how the ownership was unhappy with the imports drafted over me and would be replacing them after ONLY one scrimmage and a handful of practices, which made me understand the initial rejection, as the management clearly didn't have a clue what they were doing. Since the team was going to originally draft me before they got cold feet, I was asked to sign the biggest contract of my life and hop on a first-class flight to South Korea to play for the Ulsan Hyundai Mobis Phoebus. An emphatic "yes" was all I could muster as I made a U-Turn and headed home to pack.

Before that trip, I had never flown first class in my life. The emergency exit row and a pretty stewardess smuggling bottles of rum to me on a New Year's Eve flight in college were the closest I had been. So, sitting amongst the international elite on a thirteen hour flight was an exciting prospect. I always envisioned flying first class, sipping on champagne while a beautiful stewardess fed me lobster and grapes. This flight was nothing like that. Mainly because I wasn't drinking, as the idea of me showing up intoxicated to a job where I was already their second choice seemed unwise. Next, while the legroom was ample, the stewardesses not only didn't feed me lobster or grapes, they also didn't seem to care about the loud snoring coming from the guy whose nose resided just inches away from my ear.

I landed in Seoul, South Korea, narrowly avoiding the mad, impatient rush out of the plane, a custom which I would learn was common practice in this fast-paced culture. My handler, in this case, was a man named Jerry, who spoke very little to me during our trek out of the airport. That didn't stop me from trying to break the nervous tension, asking him every asinine, ridiculous question about Korean culture that popped into my head. His answers were short, and his patience seemed thin as we drove off to my new home.

I was under the impression that I would be headed to Ulsan, the home city of Mobis Phoebus, and a four-hour drive from the airport. I was surprised when twenty-five minutes later, we pulled up to a compound with the team logo adorning the entryway. Although my knowledge of prison was limited to the 1990 comedy, *Ernest Goes to Jail*, pulling into that compound had the distinct feeling that I was heading into imprisonment, which in a way I was. Now I have never been to prison nor committed a crime other than the occasional underage drinking or the one time I stole a pack of Bubblicious watermelon gum from the grocery store when I was seven. My mom, irate after discovering it cleverly hidden under my pillow, marched me back to the store demanding I apologize to the seventeen-year-old cashier, who I could tell gave absolutely zero craps. The Korean structure felt very confining and not at all hospitable, a place I would never hide stolen candy under my pillow for fear of being dragged out to the street and shot.

High cement fences surrounded the compound, which housed both the practice facility and the team dormitory, while a large metal gate, controlled by an armed guard, slowly opened as we pulled in. Basketball had always been fun for me. It was a game I loved to play. Within those constricting walls, it felt different. I was no longer playing this game for enjoyment; this was something else. The bleak colorless compound gave me an uneasy feeling as I was told in broken English to leave my bags in the van and only bring what's essence (must have meant, essential) to my first practice. I found out we were living around 200 miles from our arena and fan base in Ulsan. We would fly to home games and stay in a separate dormitory there. Our home games were away games because six of the ten teams in the Korean Basketball League were located within an hour's drive from Seoul. This was all explained to me, again in broken English, as I unpacked my shoes for my first practice.

I didn't unpack all my belongings in the dormitory because fellow import Keena Young and I would share an apartment a mile down the road from the training facility in Seoul. The apartment was old but had ample space and offered a much-needed escape from confinement. Our driver picked us up early in the morning, drove us at an excessive rate of speed, ran red lights, stop signs, and narrowly avoided killing pedestrians on the way to the facility. The same voyage would occur in reverse after dinner. We spent the remainder of our time in the compound, where coaches would attempt to transform my genetic composition like some sick science experiment.

I was pretty quick for a big guy. I have already discussed my transformation from a slow caterpillar into a beautiful butterfly, but apparently, I was not fast enough for my role in Korea. My role was to be that of a guard, and the powers that be decided that my joints, which are the product of thousands of years of Viking, Portuguese and Irish evolution, were destined for something more. In the year 2050, we may have bionic ligaments and tendons that would alter the athletic composition of a human being; unfortunately, at this point in 2007, such technology did not exist. I was stuck with my average length Achilles tendons. Athleticism is funny like that.

I was in the best shape of my life and more athletic than I had ever been. But there is a limit to everything, and my body was pushing that physical limit. I was drilled repeatedly, in between our mandatory three-hour practices, with quickness drills and defensive slides. When I was not on the court, I was in the weight room, performing some sort of odd lifting exercise, focused solely on my legs. Shooting, offensive moves, none of these basketball staples were practiced, only constant strain on my joints while a coach yelled in my ear, "가다!! (Go)."

The KBL held an import orientation a few weeks into our arrival. All the non-Korean players attended and were again told of all our responsibilities we now had as players in Korea. These responsibilities ranged from on and off-court obligations. When the question portion began, Corey Benjamin, the former Chicago Bull, began repeatedly asking what was going to happen to his knee. He had been drafted and subsequently injured in the preseason, replaced on the roster, but had not been paid or given the appropriate medical attention for a torn ACL. The commissioner and his lackeys began to panic, trying to get him to stop talking.

"You need to ask this question after the presentation!" the commissioner responded.

"Nah, I'm asking right now! Why won't you answer me?" Corey retaliated back.

"This is not going to be discussed during this forum!"

"WHY? Why won't you discuss it? We are all here. This has to do with everyone! I called and called, and everyone keeps passing me off. What the fuck is happening with my knee?! I need you to pay me my contract and fix my fucking knee!"

His team, Daegu Orions, had voided his contract and brought in a replacement. Benjamin, a ten-year veteran of professional basketball, deserved better. This argument went on for a few minutes. At one point, they appeared to try and have him forcefully removed before several players stood up and stepped in front of him, telling the guards to, "Back the fuck up!" This wasn't going to be an issue that would be simply swept under the rug.

The commissioner and his associates discussed in Korean while the twenty other imports sat in stunned silence. The commissioner agreed to meet with him when the orientation was over, but the damage had already been done. Was it possible this wildly organized, flashy, high-paying league could NOT actually care and void your contract if you were injured?

The season kept progressing, and my legs continued to be abused by the Mobis Phoebus coaching staff, who, despite me playing well in my normal capacities, kept trying to turn me into what I can only assume was a point guard. Late-night leg lifting sessions and agility drills turned my legs to jelly. After a while, I would show up to games with legs so fatigued it was a struggle to get out of my chair after putting my shoes on. The four to five sessions a day were taking their toll, and my performances began to suffer. The athleticism that I relied on was slowly fading.

Then it happened. At our second, my third, practice of the day, the unimaginable occurred on a play I had done over 10,000 times. I began at the wing outside the three-point line, swung the ball, and ran down to the block. Our shooter, who by now made his way into the middle of the lane, waited for me to get set so he could curl off my screen and either hit a mid-range jump shot or, if my defender helped and tried to block his shot, dump it down to me. I set my feet shoulder-width apart and angled toward his defender. He curled off beautifully, and my defender stepped up to help. As I held my position, his defender, trying to angle around me, miscalculated and his body collided hard with my knee. I had a strong base set, so when the collision occurred, my legs remained planted, and my body remained upright. My knee, however, was not so lucky, bending backward, rupturing my MCL, and slamming my femur and tibia together in a devastating impact.

Now I do not want to sound like some egotistical tough guy, but I've always had a high pain tolerance. I broke my leg in second grade when I leaped from the top of my small Catholic school's staircase, trying to imitate Luke Skywalker's refusal to accept Darth Vader as his father and fall into the inner workings of Lando Calrissian's Cloud City. Even though I had a clean break, because I was not screaming and crying, my ninety-two-year-old school nurse sent me back to class telling me that I was fine. After four hours and one first-place finish in a gym class down and back sprint, my mom noticed I was limping. She brought me to the orthopedic where my doctor marveled at the fact that I was not experiencing much pain and that I could participate in gym class with a clean break in my ankle.

When I was in college, I earned a reputation for my resilience when I played an entire season with a torn meniscus and a large chunk of bone floating under my patella. It wasn't like I couldn't feel the pain. I definitely could. I just had this issue with letting people down. I never wanted anyone who relied on me to be disappointed. I am sure there is some deep psychological reasoning behind this condition, but it allowed me to play through injuries and sickness and never be complacent. I think all the Rocky movies I watched growing up in the Philadelphia area probably had something to do with it as well.

As I sat under the basket, grasping my knee, waiting for our two incompetent trainers to make their way to my injured body, I thought about the orientation and my commitment psychosis that would not allow me to stay down. I knew this was not a smart decision, but I also knew I did not want to be sent home or let my teammates down. I hopped up and continued to practice on one knee. After practice, I went to the training room and watched as the two incompetent trainers twisted the wrong knee around while I explained multiple times, it was the other knee. I felt like I was an extra on the set of The Three Stooges while these two numbskulls pretended to be doctors. They finally grabbed my other leg and twisted it like they were trying to unscrew a soda cap causing me to scream out in pain. I explained to my translator, Lee, that something was not right with my knee. He conferred with the trainers. I had been playing for a long time, and I could tell when something was not right with my body. I knew something between my femur and my tibia and fibula was drastically wrong. This was a LEGIT injury.

My two trainers spoke to each other in Korean while occasionally looking up and pointing to my knee. The shorter one picked up his cell phone and made a call. A few minutes later, my coach walked in. My coach was not a large man; in fact, he was quite small. What he lacked in height, he made up with the ultimate male version of RBF (resting bitch face). He always looked angry, no matter what the situation. We would win a game, and he walked into the locker room like someone just kicked his dog. He was half my size, but considering I had a strong respect for authority and he controlled my future, I was a little intimidated by him. Coach joined into the knee-pointing conversation before telling me through the translator that they were sending me home right away if I was hurt.

"Am I getting surgery?" I asked my translator.

"No," he told me. "You get surgery when you arrive home." Now I was truly fucked.

In my mind, I figured if I played an entire season before on one leg, I guess I could do it again. I had no other options, either play on one leg or be sent home without my money. I chose to play. This decision would turn out to be a poor one. I limped through shoot-around the following morning with a knee brace, given to me by the shit-ass training staff, who later would pretend this interaction never happened. Applying for a medical license in South Korea must be like applying for a fishing license in the States. As long as you have a general understanding of the task and try not to hook anyone, you are granted the license.

My knee felt very unstable even with the brace, but I forged forward. Two nights later, we played in a home, but really away game, in Ulsan. I had brought with me a bottle of Advil for normal aches and pains. My thought was to numb the pain enough over the next five months; then, I could go home with all my money and let my knee rest. I took 2000mg of Advil before the game, which would turn out to be my last in Korea.

The pain medicine did its job, numbing my knee but not helping the instability I felt as if my knee would give out every time I moved laterally or horizontally. It made playing basketball quite difficult. I was on the foul line at one point and could have sworn my knee inverted like some alien in *The Arrival*.

I was not playing my best game that evening. In fact, I had not been playing my best basketball a few weeks prior. I had no excuses other than an overwhelming frustration with the constant workouts and lack of freedom. Now my knee was the major frustration as I became hesitant to cut or jump. We ended up losing that game, with much of the blame put on me. I got it. I was the import and was supposed to be the man, scoring all the points and grabbing all the rebounds. But that night, I was not physically able to handle those responsibilities.

I was discouraged and frustrated when I went to the locker room after the game ended. My translator came and grabbed me, saying the owner wanted to see me.

"What do they want?" I asked Lee.

"They just want to talk for a few minutes," he replied.

"Should I mention my knee? Will they release me if I do?"

"No. Just listen to what they say."

I walked into a smoke-filled office with the coaches and owners sitting around the darkroom staring at me. Through translation, I was asked something along the lines of "What is your problem?" Shocked by this meeting and the line of questioning, I responded by simply shrugging my shoulders. I knew if I mentioned my knee, I would be told I'm being sent home. So, I sat in silence, shrugging my shoulders and listening to the foreign language being spoken amongst them. My translator motioned to me that my portion of the meeting was over. I walked out back to the locker room to get changed and head back to the dorm.

My translator, who had a phenomenal bedside manner, stopped me at the door of the locker room and very matter of factly said, "Kevin, you have been released."

I was shocked. "Lee, are you serious?" I yelled as I stopped and turned towards him. "That was what that meeting was about? They told you that I was released?"

"Yes. You must go back to the dorm and gather your belongings."

"Lee, what about my knee? You told me not to say anything. What about my money? Am I getting surgery?"

Lee simply shrugged his shoulders. "I will find out."

My mind was racing, a common reaction to hundreds of thousands of dollars dangled over your head with no idea what would happen next. I immediately called my agent, not considering the time difference. He was very confused and not just because I woke him up in the middle of the night. "They can't do that; they have already maxed out their roster moves." A little-known rule about the KBL was that each team had an allotted two roster moves for the imports, which Hyundai Mobis Phoebus had already used. Releasing me was technically not legal. But being the laws of normal humanity and legal contracts do not apply in South Korea, I was shit out of luck. My agent told me to stay put, go back to the apartment, and he will try and sort this out.

My biggest concern now became my knee. The pain was not subsiding, and every movement was agony, shooting up and down my leg. It swelled to twice its original size. Lee called me early the next morning, telling me I needed to gather my things as they planned my flight home. "Lee, I'm not leaving until this is all situated. I need my knee fixed and my money. I am not going anywhere until that is done."

Lee told me he would call right back. Two minutes later, my phone rang again. The second I pushed the Talk button, I heard angry Korean screaming in the background, as Lee tried his best to keep up. It was my coach. He informed me that I would need to report to the gym to run sprints for twenty-four hours straight if I did not sign off on my release.

"Lee, I can't run with my knee right now. I am not running for twenty-four hours. That is fucking crazy!"

The screaming became more intense, and Lee raised his voice just to keep up with the chaos, screamed, "If you do not report, you are in breach of contract, and we will release you without your consent!"

Lee promptly hung up the phone. I became speechless. I looked at my roommate Keena Young and explained what just occurred. He reminded me of what happened in orientation with Corey Benjamin and that I need to go to the KBL office and make a scene. "I don't think they will care," I said. "The reason they talked to Corey was because we were all there, and they couldn't escort him out or ignore him."

I again called my agent, interrupting his sleep for the second straight evening. "Mike, they are trying to make me run sprints until I agree to the release."

"Just hang tight, let me talk to them," he replied.

I had heard horror stories about overseas players having their contracts suddenly and illegally voided. If the player refused to leave, they were threatened similarly. One player in Europe was told flat out that if he did not leave, the team would plant drugs somewhere in his apartment and then promptly call the police like a scene from the movie *Brokedown Palace*. The player reluctantly agreed with fear of false imprisonment. This was/is how some teams operate, creating a my-word-against-your-word situation.

Mike called me back, and I could tell immediately that the conversation was not going to be a good one. "Kevin, you are going to have to come home."

"What about my knee? Who is fixing this?" I asked.

He explained that they would be held responsible for all my medical bills, and if the injury were deemed severe enough to keep me out for an extended period of time, I would receive the rest of my contract. Later that day, Jerry Lee, who was the other translator and had more of a management position with the team, brought me a piece of paper that said I was being released and asked me to sign it. I wasn't ok with the wording throughout the document. So I added all the information on my injury and my situation underneath their typed nonsense. I'm sure that document was promptly shredded, and my signature forged shortly after walking out of the room.

I prepped for my departure from South Korea. Again, before boarding the plane, I looked that fucking snake Jerry Lee directly into his eyes and verified that Mobis Phoebus would cover my medical expenses and pay me my money, or in layman's terms, honor my contract. My grandfather once told me only a snake looks you in the eyes and lies. Jerry looked me in the eyes and lied. I had assurances from all personnel and the addendum on the release they gave me that my situation would be successfully resolved. I felt that legally I had protected myself enough. I stepped onto the plane and flew out of hell.

Shortly after arriving home, I visited the orthopedist who, not surprisingly, told me my knee was seriously injured. I sent my MRI along with my orthopedist's write up on the injury to Jerry Lee, and the rest of the Mobis Phoebus high brass, who responded with an email, pretending this was the first they heard of it:

"In the case of Kevin's knee, he didn't say anything about it when he was here. Trainer asked him about his body condition several times, but Kevin said he had no problem. Ask him. I don't think it is our responsibility. -Jerry"

My agent responded: "Kevin's knee is still extremely swollen. He has gotten an MRI since arriving home (at his own expense), which he was told to do before he left Korea but was never given a chance. He injured his knee on Monday, November 5th. He received treatment on it in Ulsan every day until his release. He played through the pain on Wednesday's game wearing a knee brace given to him by the training staff. That alone makes it sound as if the trainers knew of his injury.

All we ask is that Mobis do the right thing. Kevin is paying for medical expenses that should be taken care of by the team. Kevin is keeping his certified medical records and receipts and can easily send them to you for reimbursement. Please advise."

Jerry Lee responded with: "What you wrote is just your guess that is based on your experience, which is not true. If Kevin told us about his pain, we could replace him by injury without any penalty. Please ask Kevin once again about it. Actually, Kevin's playing was not an issue for coach at that time. There was no reason for us to force him to play with injury."

Now Jerry and I discussed this multiple times, including right before I boarded the plane. He also has shitty grammar for a translator. I don't even know where to start. And as for the truth, it's easy to accuse someone of lying when their knee isn't swollen to the size of a grapefruit. This back-and-forth denial went on for some time. I filed a lawsuit before I was advised that it would be tried in South Korea, and the chances of success were extremely low, as loyalty lies deeper than law.

Meanwhile, I rehabbed my knee daily to maintain a shot of playing again in a few months. Two months after Korea, I was offered an incredible contract from the Australian NBL, the same league I played in the year before, for a rival team, the New Zealand Breakers. I was not cleared to play for another three months and had to decline. I had to pass on going back to paradise because my knee was still fucked. Allow me to recap: my knee was screwed up, I was living in my parent's attic, passing on high-paying jobs, paying all my medical expenses, and rehabbing in order for me to try and reignite my career.

Hyundai Mobis Phoebus took a great deal from me but looking back, I relished the opportunity. I worked my ass off to get a spot, and I worked my ass off to maintain it. I was unfortunate to be injured and more unfortunate to be fucked over by people I trusted. This experience taught me a great deal about how some organizations are poorly managed. It was useful information as I continued my career and life, where I will forever boycott all Hyundai products. #sorrynotsorry

Chapter 8

Lording Over the Rings

I was not a fan of change. It always took me a while to adjust to new situations. Even from a young age, I liked routine, which is why I had the same haircut from the age of eight to twenty-two: a trim on the top with a two on the side. When I finally grew my hair out my senior year in college, I could only maintain it for half the year since the adjustment became too much for my shower routine. Eventually, I adapted and accepted the changes in my life. It wasn't always easy, especially as my career progressed and I had to adjust to different countries, teams, fans, coaches and players. Which was why I was so surprised to be doing shots at three o'clock in the morning with the entire Wellington Saints team after arriving in New Zealand only eight hours prior.

The time immediately before my arrival was spent living in the attic of my childhood home. I had been rehabbing my knee for five months after being ghosted by the Korean Basketball League. There was something very uneasy about living with your parents at twenty-eight-years-old. It had a definite Will Ferrell *Wedding Crashers* vibe to it. It was not something I aspired to do after writing *Professional Basketball Player* on my tax forms the year before. The stigma of living with your parents at that age was both embarrassing and depressing.

I had garnered loads of interest from the Southern Hemisphere after my lone Australian season and was offered a contract by the Wellington Saints of the New Zealand Basketball League. I called my orthopedic to get clearance on my knee. Dr. Torpe, the longtime mender of my joints, told me there was only one way to find out. After five months of physical therapy and one week on the court, I once again took off on an insanely long, fear-filled flight to the land of Mordor, Rivendell and The Shire.

There are very few jobs where you can be offered a contract then flown halfway around the world sight unseen. However, that is exactly what happens with overseas basketball. Some grainy footage and the word of your agent is all it takes for teams to offer you tons of money and an international flight. Upon arriving at your Tinder-like date, sometimes you are not their cup of tea and labeled return to sender. This is why they pay for just a single round-trip ticket so they can survey you. If there is a match, they fly any other important family member over. Because of this common scenario, I headed to New Zealand solo, without my wife, who remained in the attic of my childhood home.

I arrived in Nelson, New Zealand, a small town on the southern island just a few hours before the Saints took on the Nelson Giants. Since I had been traveling for thirty-one straight hours and was exhausted, I was not making my playing debut that night. Instead, I would be watching the game from the bench in street clothes. My anxiety was already fairly high, as this was the first time I ever watched a game from the stands while playing overseas. I was going through the usual stressors: *Would my teammates like me? Were they going to be pissed that I wasn't playing? Why did I decide to wear flip-flops with this outfit? My toes are freezing.* These thoughts danced through my head as I sat behind the bench, watching my new team warm up.

Before tipoff, my new teammates, one by one, made their way over to introduce themselves, starting with my former Cairns

Taipan point guard, Luke Martin, who I already knew well, followed by a former opponent in the NBL, Nick Horvath. Nick and I played in the All-Star game a year earlier and hung out a bit during All-Star Weekend but were not personally close. This would soon change as we bro hugged, and Nick told me how excited he was that we were now teammates. I sat on the bench, alternating between clapping and trying not to doze off, as I had slept only three or four hours during the voyage.

The game ended, and my excitement for a warm bed that I would be sleeping in alone was more than it should have been. I was walking through the hotel lobby, half asleep, when Nick walked up to me. "Hey, KO, let's go. We are heading out for a drink."

I was torn between getting acquainted with my pillow or my new teammates. I was remarkably sleep-deprived and barely functioning, but at the same time, I wanted to bond with the team. I began scanning my brain, calculating how many hours I could stay awake before dying. It was a decision that would change the entire dynamic of my stay. *Don't be weird, Kevin! Go!*

"Sure," I said, as I turned around and headed out with Nick and Luke to the waiting cab. "Is there a place to get coffee or something?" I asked on the drive. "I'm so tired."

Nick smiled in a way I would become familiar with. That smile meant he had some sort of ludicrous plan that would most likely end up hurting me. "First thing we'll order when we get to the bar."

We arrived at a large club with music that seemed to amplify my headache. Shortly after, the rest of the team joined us. They praised me for fighting through my insomnia. Nick walked up to the bar.

"Four Red Bull vodkas," he told the bartender.

"Coffee, huh? I said.

Nick nodded and downed the one drink. "The rest is for you," he told me, sliding the other three drinks in front of me. "Down the hatch, KO! This is how we do it in NZ. You're a Kiwi now."

I took a deep breath and, one by one, drank them down. My body began to shake, a combination of malnutrition, fatigue and the Red Bull, which made my heartbeat at an unhealthy pace. "Holy Shit," I said as my eyes grew wider. "Is this what drugs are like? I feel like I can run a marathon right now."

Nick looked at me and grinned, "Now we're talking."

I was thoroughly introduced to everyone that night, starting with Ernest Scott, a fellow American, who would count as our other import since Nick was about to become a naturalized New Zealand citizen. The rest of the team was incredibly welcoming, including Brendon Pongia. Along with being our veteran presence, he was also the host of Good Morning, the country's premier morning news program. Each new introduction was met with another round of drinks. We were two hours into being a team, and I felt like I knew them my whole life.

Now, I had been to many lands and drank in many bars, but I never saw a group take over an establishment as I did in New Zealand. Our physiotherapist, Gavin Cross, a former British military man and incredibly awesome badass, lined up a round of shots. "To KO!" he shouted as everyone raised their drinks. "Hopped off the plane with no hesitation and is getting absolutely smashed!"

Everyone shouted and downed their shots. Nick looked at me, "KO," he said, "You are not sleeping tonight."

Every time it looked like my eyes were closing, a drink was shoved in my face as several members of the team jumped up and down around me. It was like some sort of incredible torture. I was being sleep-deprived but in the most enjoyable way possible. Things continued to get progressively worse before my body gave in and I was out. Luckily, I was close to my hotel room and was able to be thrown into bed. My next conscious thought was from the airport at six o'clock in the morning as we boarded a short flight back to Wellington.

This kind of behavior would become a trend during my time with the Kiwis. On the court, I worked harder than I ever worked before, and off the court, I partied harder than I ever had before. I know that is probably not something to brag about, as people see athletes partying too much as a flaw but fuck all that. Athletes perform better when they are happy, and in New Zealand, I was truly happy. I experienced life like I never experienced before, and it all started on the court.

In the past, when a contract was sent to me, it was based on a monthly salary. You will play from August through May and make X amount of dollars per month. That would then force me to use the math skills I swore I would never need after struggling to understand what a matrice was in college. Add up the months, and that is the take-home pay, in most cases. In other instances, divide by two, then kick yourself in the balls, and there is your total. My contract with the Saints was different. Sure, there was the monthly salary, but this contract was the first time I would receive a bonus. I don't know if my agent did some backroom dealings or if the team just wanted to give me an extra incentive to be a rebounding machine. Regardless, I was given a $150 bonus for every game that I achieved a double-double, which is ten or more points and ten or more rebounds.

This extra bit of money fueled my drive, well, that and Nick Horvath. We crossed paths as opponents in the Australian NBL, me with the Taipans and him with the Adelaide 36ers, and five years earlier when we were both lowly college students. Nick was a Blue Devil from one of the most hated/beloved college programs in the world and my 2001 NCAA Tournament opponent, Duke University. Nick was a star and had the work ethic to match. He had won the 1999 Minnesota Mr. Basketball, then played under the tutelage of Coach Mike Krzyzewski. He had learned from the best and had a wide knowledge of the game. I came from the underdog mentality. Fighting tooth and nail for everything I had, barely scraping by but never really knowing exactly what I was doing. Together, our powers created a supernova of tireless effort that would propel us to the top of the standings.

Every day after practice concluded, I would lay on the floor stretching my tired muscles. Nick would walk up to me and say something absurd like "C'mon, KO, defensive slide suicides," as he smiled a devious smile which meant he was concocting some other form of torture for us.

"Alright," I would say, shaking my head. "Let's go." My competitive juices tended to get in the way of the pain still lingering in my right knee. I would stick around after practice in past seasons to get shots up or perfect something I was struggling with. I can honestly say I never stayed after to do defensive slide suicides, or medicine ball runs, or backboard touches unless I was being punished; that was until I arrived in New Zealand.

But that was our dynamic. Nick and I played similar positions; both 7-footers (with shoes on) would battle every day. Those battles were never peaceful as we would go at each other's throats. Occasionally, I would get the best of Nick, and occasionally he would get the best of me, which would result in me punching the hardwood floor with both fists as hard as I could because I was a fucking baby. Immediately all eyes in the gym would turn to me in horror, watching this barbaric display. I was a little surprised by their shock, as New Zealand was the land of the Haka, a Maori ceremonial dance where scary-looking jacked people smack their hands against their elbow, chest and thighs all while screaming and stomping. It is an intimidating ritual that strikes fear in the hearts of opponents.

While the people of New Zealand have the Haka, an important part of their heritage, I had barehanded floor punching, an important part of mine. The ability to punch the floor at full force without causing any damage to my hands, wrists or arms. Once I realized I could do this technique perfectly without harm, I began slowly increasing the force until I was punching the floor with both hands as hard as I could, causing the wood to shake. My knuckles have since created a hard layer of scar tissue, making them look bonier than usual. Nick loved the floor punch, as it let him know he was getting the best of me, and also because I did it a lot and never even had a bruise.

I never came up with the ideas in which we would torture ourselves after practice. I left that up to Nick and his brilliant mind. You see, he was also given the same bonus incentive I was. The team ownership must have decided to flood the rebounding market, assuming since there were now two of us fighting for extra cash, the Saints would lead the league in rebounds. Assuming, though, that they would only have to pay one of us, as the likelihood of us both getting a double-double every game was low. That hypothesis was proven only partially correct. While we did lead the league in rebounding that year, they incorrectly predicted they would be out only $150 a game. Nick and I got that bonus EVERY FUCKING GAME. Black eyes, bruises, stitches, it didn't matter. We would fight like wild dogs for every single rebound. Some nights Nick and I out-rebounded entire teams by ourselves.

This money would then be spent later that night when we would all hit up downtown Wellington to party. It would start with a few snake bites, a combination of lager and cider, then a few shots, a few more snake bites, a lot more shots, and then the team taking our shirts off at the bar and getting loud and rowdy until we eventually stumbled to our homes and passed out. We called this trend halvsies, and it happened way more than you would expect a group of professional adults to take their shirts off in crowded bars.

I never loved taking my shirt off early in life, mainly because I looked like Christian Bale from *The Machinist* when I did. At the pool growing up, I would fold my arms across my chest and stick both hands behind my biceps, giving the appearance of extra mass. This served the purpose of pretending the two skinny noodles hanging off my shoulders were muscular, and the folded arms allowed me to cover up my bird chest. Gavin Cross fixed all of that. Gavin, our team physiotherapist, treated our injuries but was also a renowned fitness instructor who, after Nick and I thoroughly tortured ourselves at practice, brought me to the weight room to create functional strength.

I was strong, and I had packed on muscle since my youth, but I was never Gerard Butler in *300* jacked. I was either too skinny or big, but not defined. Gavin introduced me to a new way of training. My body would be a combination of, I can't do another rep, and I'm going to throw up at the end of every workout. It concluded each week with the three of us doing the actual *300* Workout together. This workout was the same routine Butler and the rest of the cast endured to convey what 300 Spartans looked like holding off Persians at the Hot Gates with ridiculously defined six-packs covered in some kind of ancient baby oils. While my body was not yet screen-ready, it was worthy of popping my shirt off in a crowded bar. From the time I arrived, my basketball body and basketball mindset had gone through a complete overhaul in this beautiful island nation.

New Zealand is beautiful. It still, to this day, is the most radiant, serene place I have ever encountered. Most of my previous travels took me to incredible man-made structures that I read about in history books, but there was nothing to prepare me for the natural beauty of this land. New Zealand is unique. While having a similar square mileage to the state of Colorado, from town to town, the landscape is completely different. Auckland has a metropolitan feeling and is just an hour's drive to a lush area, greener than any high-definition television could project. Another hour takes you to incredible beaches, lined with surfers, just a short distance away from stunning mountain ranges. A trip to the South Island surrounds you with crystal clear rivers, volcanos, hot pools and rainforests.

During my four-month stay, I took many day trips to see this magnificent terrain firsthand. I was also able to geek out at several of the filming locations for *Lord of the Rings*. If I had my collection of swords, I would have cosplayed the shit out of those locations, dressing up like Aragorn or, better yet, one of the Nazgûl, the black-robed riders, that tried unsuccessfully to kill the whiney hobbits throughout three movies. Even without the costumes, these day trips were an exciting experience. At Mt. Victoria just outside of Wellington, I hid in the embankment where the hobbits hid as the Black Riders approached. Fun dork fact, the tree with the huge roots was not there. It was a prop made specifically for the movie. I did, however, lay around the spot where that scene was filmed being stared at by locals.

I took some of the trips alone, wandering through these natural wonders, clearing my mind of any stress from basketball. I would sometimes sit on the dock behind our arena and stare out into the Cook Strait that separates the two islands. It was a surreal mental experience. Writer Jean-Christophe Rufin talked about nature's ability to heal one's mind. "It takes away all vanity from the mind and all suffering from the body, it removes the rigid shell that surrounds all things and separates them from our consciousness; it brings the self into harmony with nature." I had gone full-on Phil Jackson.

Oh, and I also played some basketball there as well against some big dudes. Every team on the schedule had a monstrous human that could probably stomp my head in, then beat me at one on one, most notably, Pero Cameron. Cameron gained international recognition as he led the New Zealand National Team, known as the Tall Blacks, to the semifinals of the 2002 FIBA World Championships. Pero is also a mountain of a man. Playing against him was like playing against Thanos. No matter how heroic and strong you thought you were, he was always prepared to snap you from existence.

The rest of the league was just as rugged. Imagine professional basketball meets a men's league. Some guys were young and trying to make it to the big leagues in Australia, and some guys were at the twilight of their career, a little out of shape, a step slower, but neutralizing their declining athleticism with brute force. It was like taking a time machine back to the NBA in the late 80s. There were no easy layups, and fouls were earned by throwing opponents to the ground. The physicality of this league was intense. You had to work for every single point, which is why the extra effort I exerted after practice was so beneficial.

New Zealand was a basketball and spiritual awakening for me. I finally took the time to read several classical novels I told my collegiate professors I already read. I hiked up a mountain and drove from the passenger side of my car over an extremely narrow cliff to see a beach inhabited by thousands of seals. Another fun dork fact for you: seals smell really bad. I do not know why I was expecting anything different from an animal that eats fish, swims in the ocean, then lays in the hot sun, but the stench was overpowering. My goal was to see one of these adorable creatures being consumed by a large Orca, which was known to prey on the slower swimmers just a few meters from shore. But due to the smell and impatience, I only stayed for a short time before hopping back into the car and making the perilous journey back to stable land.

I began to think philosophically and embraced the struggles of my life while cherishing the triumphs—my mental focus on working out and playing the game improved as well. I watched videos of Hakeem Olajuwon and Kevin McHale. I practiced their signature moves over and over until I perfected them in a game. I would then brag that I hit someone with a Dream Shake or a Slippery Eel. In New Zealand, I was the healthiest, happiest and most authentic me. My hair grew down to my shoulders, my beard grew beyond just stubble, and I embraced the beast that lurked inside my mind. It was me—the me I always wished to be. After such a horrible experience in South Korea, this journey allowed me to refocus and balance the ups and downs of professional basketball. As a Japanese philosopher once said, "You must take the good with the bad, smile with the sad. Love what you got and remember what you had. Always forgive, but never forget, learn from your mistakes but never regret it. People change, things go wrong, but just remember life goes on."

My life had received a much-needed tune-up. I just did not realize how quickly the gears would again fall off, and the "L" in luck would be replaced with an "F."

Chapter 9

Those Crazy Balkans

Why does he keep looking back here? I kept shifting my legs, encompassing a large portion of my 6-foot 10-inch frame, to the other side of my cramped coach seat. *Does he want to see me struggle? Maybe he hates tall people.* The older man just stared, with his stubby legs barely reaching the floor of his spacious emergency exit seat, the most coveted seat for all international basketballers. I hated him. I did not know him, and I don't hate anyone, but I hated him. *Smug bastard.* Sickened by his stupid face, I glanced out the window as we descended below the clouds.

The picturesque landscape of the Swiss Alps I admired on our ascent was replaced by something completely different. We soared over land, still feeling the effect of war twenty years prior. Craters could be seen from a half-mile up scattered between the remnants of the Balkan Mountains. Broken-down buildings and villages abandoned and destroyed littered the countryside as we slowly approached Prishtina, Kosovo.

The plane landed at an airport not much larger than the one I made for my GI Joes in the backyard growing up. The plane had to brake so hard to stay on the runway without plowing into the grass. My Dell mp3 player went flying out of my hands, sliding to the feet of the man four rows in front of me. I uncoiled my legs from the cramped seat, collected my belongings, and disembarked from the plane, making sure to ignore the requests for assistance from the older man now reaching for the overhead with his dickhead stubby arms.

I made my way into the airport terminal, which consisted of a few airport hangers, one restaurant and a small magazine stand. I walked the short distance through the airport towards the baggage claim to meet up with the team's gopher sent to pick up the tallest man at the airport.

Usually, a sign was waiting for me with my name on it. In Australia, the sign was bedazzled with the team's logo, making me feel like the man. As my bags were scooped up, I was escorted to a beautiful vehicle, a Five Star dinner and a condo in a tropical resort. Other times my name was yelled in a broken English accent "Ovens, Meesta Ovens." Other times like in Kosovo, I walked off the plane past the four people waiting for loved ones, and to the baggage claim. There I stood waiting, not only for anyone who may know why a man of my impressive physique may be at the airport but for my luggage as well.

The baggage monster, which vomits out countless identical black Samsonite suitcases, had finished its upheaval, yet my life resting in two ironically, matching black pieces of Samsonite luggage was lost. It was a nightmare. The bags contained all the earthly possessions I deemed valuable at the time. Not only my clothing and basketball gear but my PlayStation as well. Any globetrotting pro will tell you that a video game console is undoubtedly the most important item to bring. Nothing breaks up the monotonous boredom of a nine-month stay in a foreign country like twelve-hour binges of Grand Theft Auto. Now, these young cats bring a system and an iPad and call it a day. But back in my day, a bulky laptop, a video game console, two large booklets of DVDs and a portable mouse weighed down my suitcase. These items had all vanished into the cold, bleak Kosovan morning.

As I stood at the conveyor belt, alone and more than a little freaked out, an older man with a scar on his face and a lit cigarette hanging out of his mouth approached me.

"You here for ze racquet?" the scary Albanian asked in broken English. I stared at him with a blank expression. "Racquet?!" He began making a shooting motion with his hands.

"Yes, Sir, I am. I just was signed for Sigal Prishtina."

"Ahh!" He proceeded to walk away.

What the hell was that? I stood alone in this foreign airport, being stared at by two security guards carrying large automatic weapons and looking at me suspiciously. They occasionally whispered to one another and then glared in unison. I stood there for another five minutes, wondering how much my harvested organs would go for on the black market. Then a different older man with a cigarette hanging from his mouth came up to me, and in better English, asked if Arben had told me to come to the car. I assumed the frightening individual with the scar was Arben. I replied, "No sir, Arben neglected to mention anything other than the assumption I played racquetball. Oh, and, funny story, my luggage is missing."

The new cigarette-smoking old man nodded his head with a slight smirk, then shook my hand, introducing himself, oddly enough, also as Arben, telling me to stay put. He confidently strolled over to the two gun-toting men standing by the security checkpoint whispering to each other. There was some finger-wagging and loud exchanges that did nothing to settle my ever-growing anxiety. Now, if the countless episodes of *The A-Team* taught me anything, it was never, ever yell and initiate a physical confrontation with a man holding a gun. But that is precisely what New Arben did, screaming at the one angry guard and pointing at me. Finally, one of the men walked into the back and emerged with my luggage. New Arben walked my bags over to me, winked and said, "See, No problem."

I had no idea why my bags were held in a shady backroom, especially since I had already cleared customs in Switzerland. My mind raced, thinking about every item in my bag that could have been considered illegal in this new land. Regardless, whether they were watching movies on my laptop or seriously did plan to sell all my belongings once they killed me, I had my possessions and felt some sense of relief.

The feeling was short-lived as I walked out to the snow-filled parking lot and waited for a vehicle that would take me to my destination. A small silver sedan pulled in front of me with New Arben and Other Arben sitting in the front. I tossed my bags into the old jalopy, sat in the back, and refocused on the main reason I was there, to play basketball. I began to think about the team. *How should I acclimate myself? What role would I play?* A loud crash interrupted my thought process. We had driven from the pavement of the airport parking lot to an actual DIRT ROAD that would lead us to the capital of Kosovo. My basketball concerns quickly became concerns for something completely different. I stared out the window, looking past the bomb-made craters, and wondered what I had gotten myself into.

Just days before, I had signed a contract with the top team in Kosovo, Sigal Prishtina, after a contract from Sweden fell through. I did very little research on the Balkan country, knowing only the basic location of my new home and their unassuming fans. Unassuming. That is the best way to describe the Albanian Hooligans that followed the Sigal Prishtina Basketball Team around Kosovo. During the day, they were normal. On game day, they became homicidal maniacs. I remember being introduced to them shortly after I arrived in Kosovo. I was brought into a dimly lit smoke-filled bar filled with about six more Arbens and was seated at a back table. I could feel the glare of the patrons as I sat quietly with my recently found luggage. The smoke created a fog so thick I wasn't sure if I were in Kosovo or the protagonist in an Edgar Allen Poe story.

A man walked up to the table and asked, in some form of broken English, if I was hungry. I nodded politely. He then disappeared behind a closed door. Minutes later, plates of food were placed in front of me by several members of the staff. Some foods looked quasi familiar, while some looked completely foreign. I decided to stick with what I sort of knew and nibbled on the chicken wings and bread. After only a few short minutes, the staff reemerged and completely cleared the table while I was in midchew. I quickly tossed a half-eaten wing onto one of the rapidly disappearing plates as the table was wiped clean. I felt like I was taking a ride on the Polar Express.

Several figures emerged from the dense fog that surrounded me and sat down. All of them had lit cigarettes resting comfortably on their lips. "I am Arben, your coach," muttered the tallest individual. *Another Arben, this must be a joke.* I have several close friends named Mike, and never in my life had they all been in the same place at the same time. But here I sat, with seven Arbens surrounding me, all chain-smoking cigarettes, while slowly giving me emphysema.

After Coach Arben gave me the rundown on the logistics of my stay, Ymer, the fan group leader, lit a cigarette, placed his lighter on the table, and stared into my soul. "We are champions, Kevin," he stated. "Not just last year, and the year before that, but this year as well. We will win another championship this year, and you are here to help us do that."

I sipped on my water, nodding my head and hoping this situation would end quickly, much like when I was fifteen, and my mom found six empty Foster bottles hidden under my bed and reamed me out for several hours. Fosters, Australian for grounded.

This would be one of many odd interactions during my first day in Kosovo. After being thoroughly intimidated, I was told to gather my belongings and follow them. I walked down the street, carting all my heavy luggage behind me, hoping that I was being led to a car. Instead, they brought me through the hallways of a small mall, which led to our arena. "This is where you play!" Arben told me. I was quickly whisked away to the locker room. Two of my new teammates sat putting on their shoes.

"Hello," Edmond, the caption of the team, greeted me in perfect English. "Welcome to the team. Do not use the shower." He then walked away, leaving me with far more questions than I already had.

Coach Arben shook his head in agreement while I sat dumbfounded. "Put your gear on for practice." Coach then followed Edmond out. I stood in the locker room with a young-looking teammate who I could tell spoke no English and smiled at me, nodding his head repeatedly. I opened my bags on the dirty floor and rooted through the tightly packed clothing to find my gear.

I ran through the rigmarole of normal practice, learned some plays and made some shots, then put on my hoodie as I was again told to follow with my heavy bags in tow. We ended up across the street in front of various storefronts. It was dark, and most of the businesses were closed for the evening. We arrived at a dark black gate, which led to a dark hallway. "Here is apartment," Coach said to me as I stared into the darkness. As if he was a nocturnal creature, he began racing through the darkness and up a flight of stairs. I could see the glow of cigarette embers as I reached the top of the landing. A man stood outside the door nodding at me in a not too friendly manner.

"This is where you live," Coach informed me as we stopped at the door directly across from the odd man—*the neighbors already like me.* Coach Arben disappeared into the darkness after handing me the key. I opened the door, placed my belongings down and began my life in Kosovo.

I spent my time off the court getting to know the nuances of the Balkan territory while occasionally being summoned to weird meetings like my intro to the fans. There were things in Pristina I never experienced before in my career, like sitting alone in the dark during the frequent power outages. Or making sure I took my shower and brushed my teeth before eleven o'clock at night when the entire country's water supply shut down for the night. It was something I found out firsthand when I was sudsed up mid-shower and the water suddenly stopped. These fun facts remained excluded from the internet searches I did before leaving.

On the court, I reunited with Hyundai Mobis Phoebus teammate Keena Young, who, along with the University of Wyoming standout Brad Jones, would provide me with some sense of normalcy as we shared in the off and on unintentional comedy show that was Kosovo basketball. A sarcastic Jim from *The Office* glance was a common occurrence as the insanity around us unfolded. Case and point, our trip to the Kosovo All-Star Game.

It was a pretty big deal, as the three of us were all selected to play, representing the International Team. With every All-Star game, there was some sort of grandeur that accompanied the honor. In high school, I was given a jersey with my name on the back and a bag of gear. In college, there was an award show with plaques and expensive food. And Australia made an entire weekend out of the experience, flying me to Adelaide for a stay at a fancy hotel, accompanied by parties, dinners, bonuses and gear.

Our traveling party to the game consisted of Keena, Brad, our coach Arben Krasniqi, our captain Edmond Azemi and me. We met at the gym in the morning for our three-hour trip to Therandë, the town where the game would be held. I do not know exactly what I was expecting in Kosovo, but it did lack the glitz and glam I became accustomed to in the past. I assumed there would be some sort of pomp and circumstance to this day. I figured we would have something comfortable and fancy to transport us to the game. I was caught off guard when a green minivan circa 1984 pulled up. The engine puttered, and the rust eating away at the lower exterior was very noticeable. It was also not very big, so fitting five oversized humans and a driver comfortably was impossible. I glanced up at Keena, who simply shook his head. We sardined ourselves into the tiny van in hopes that it would make it to our destination. I did not realize the irony of my sarcasm at the time.

We were, what I can only assume to be, halfway between Pristina and Therandë when our driver, who for some reason had decided not to fill up on gas before leaving the city, pulled into a small service area. The popping in my ears had subsided as we passed through a mountain range and back to sea level.

Now let me paint you a picture of Kosovo. There are cities located sporadically throughout the country. These cities are connected by bleak, dark, empty roads, not major highways or interstates. The gas station was in the middle of nowhere with nothing but open snowy fields for miles. I shoehorned my way out into the cold air and stretched my legs as the attendant began filling up the tank.

A minute later, the man pumping the gas put both hands on his head and shouted "QIJ! (Albanian swear word)," and disappeared into the small building. Another worker walked out with him just seconds later, muttering something as he made his way over to the van. Our driver, who had been muttering back and forth with our coach, began raising his voice towards the two men. The shouting grew more intense when our coach, who held one hand on his head, and the other stretched straight out in front, began screaming at the attendants as well. The two employees evened out the odds and began screaming back at them. I stood watching four grown men yelling at each other, with both their mouths and hands, for six to seven minutes on a secluded road with no other structure in sight. And then it began to snow, heavily.

"What is happening, Edmond?" I asked a little unnerved, as crazy people pulling out weapons over innocent disputes happened more than you would think in Kosovo.

"He put diesel into the engine instead of normal petrol. I don't think the engine will start now."

While I was not an expert on car engines, I assumed having the wrong gas pumping through the combustion chamber may have some negative consequences, especially with a vehicle I am pretty sure I heard coughing on the first half of the drive.

"Does anyone know how to fix this?" Keena asked. Edmond shrugged and joined into the angry Albanian argument.

The worst part about this situation was that being halfway to our destination it would take an hour and a half for anyone to reach us with a new shitty minivan to complete the trip. I quickly surveyed the parking lot, looking for ulterior modes of transportation. Nothing! Just two bikes that I assumed belonged to the two workers who were currently participating in the screaming match. Considering what we drove thus far, hopping on a bike for the remainder of the trip would not be much of a downgrade.

One of the employees finally broke away from the shouting, grabbed a large pan then crawled under the van. The rest of us stood outside in the cold blizzard waiting for this to be sorted out. There was quite a bit of muffled Albanian swearing, followed by the banging together of metal and the occasional ping of an important engine part falling off the van and hitting the concrete. He emerged fifteen minutes later covered in all sorts of filth, with a pan filled with diesel fuel.

The original fuck up employee took the fuel nozzle and placed it back into the van. Before he could begin pumping, the now filthy man who drained the engine smacked him across the back of the head and shoved him out of the way. One hour from when we stopped, the engine fired up, and we were back on our way to the All-Star Game. While batshit crazy in my mind, this was just a minor hiccup that season. We would win a game and something absurd would happen. Brad, Keena and I would look at each other frustrated and then it would repeat all over again. We rolled through the league that year, not losing a single game in the regular season, which is why it was so confusing that our fans remained restless. Sigal Prishtina was the top team in Kosovo, and any close win was met with anger from the fans.

This brings me to the half-court of Karagaç Sports Hall in Peja, Kosovo, and the final of the Kosovo Cup. I stood there as the ringing in my ears grew louder and louder. I tried to regather my senses amid the solid run by the home team Peja against my team Sigal Prishtina.

The fans from both teams screamed at deafening decibels. They were separated into two balconies overlooking the court on opposite ends. Fans were only able to reach the opposing section by entering through the exterior door designed just for that specific fan base. Or by trying to scale the wall like Spiderman and climb across to the opposite balcony. Surprisingly one fan already had attempted to do so before being ripped from the wall by the riot gear donning police force below. Another way was to have a bunch of the larger fans slowly lower you down so you can run directly across the court, then fire a flare directly into the heart of the opposing fans, which, NOT surprisingly, had been attempted twice.

The deafening noise was like nothing I heard in all my years of basketball. The fans had been creating a raucous environment all night. But at this moment, my eardrums could not handle the screaming of the Peja fans, and it was about to get worse. As I stood disoriented at half-court, our team was struggling to break Peja's aggressive press. Suddenly the ball came to me. I could blame it on the noise, or the fans, or the piece of foam that covered my headphones, thus not exposing me to the noise of that magnitude growing up. Regardless, I quickly turned the ball over. The Peja crowd somehow grew louder. I was shell-shocked. My head was spinning, and my eardrums were about to burst. Thankfully, our coach called timeout, giving us a chance to get reacclimated with normal volume levels.

The timeout worked. We quickly built a solid lead that propelled us to the win and the Kosovo Cup. As the minutes ticked down, both sets of fans stayed in their sections, continuing to bang drums relentlessly and light flares, which created a haze of smoke on the court. In most situations, fans would start making their way to the exits to beat traffic or be the first guy at the bar. But not here, not in Karagaç Sports Hall in Peja. The fans had something else in store for us. Angry that the Cup was out of reach, Peja fans began to pull different items out of their pockets, which would be useful at a Soc/Greaser rumble rather than a basketball game.

My captain ran up to me and yelled in broken English, "Kevin, when ten seconds left, you follow me to bench as fast as you can!" I sensed the seriousness in his voice and the urgency in his eyes, leading me to believe they would not be pouring Gatorade over my head in celebration.

The flares that had been lit and extinguished all evening now created a raging red fire in the middle of the Prishtina balcony. This was soon matched by a large sea of red fire from the Peja fans. It was their barbaric battle cry. *I have more fire than you and, therefore, must be far more superior.* Suddenly, a single stick of red fire that had resided, not all that safely in the balconies, flew over our heads, giving a bright red glow to the scoreboard that still read thirty-eight seconds. The accuracy of this toss led me to believe we would not be seeing an elite pitcher from the Balkan region anytime soon. It was thrown with too much loft, hitting the roof and plummeting back to earth in a comet of red. The destination of that fire stick, unfortunately, was directly onto the playing floor. In a situation like this in any other basketball game in any other country, world, or galaxy, the players would be immediately ushered off the court and into the safe confines of the locker room. Here however, the referee picked up the lit flare that was now littering the court and calmly tossed it to the sidelines while the game continued.

Praying that this nightmare would soon be over, I instructed our point guard to "HOLD THE FUCKING BALL!" Now whether his English was not terrific, or he was trying to pad his stats, our young guard drove into the lane and was fouled, sending him to the line for two shots. The growing sea of fire continued as I looked up at the clock, which still read seventeen seconds. I assumed my spot on the bottom block as we lined up for a free throw and the Peja fans lined up my head for target practice. After the second shot rattled in, a large coin rattled off the bottom of the backboard, just inches away from my head, the whistle blew. *Thank God! They are calling the game for safety concerns.* Nope, I was wrong. The Peja coach had inexplicably called a timeout. There was nothing to discuss as our double-digit lead would not evaporate in the last few seconds of the game. It seemed more of a ploy for the Peja fans to continue their aerial assault on the group of twenty-somethings that were simply there for athletic competition.

Our coach was irate, screaming at the Peja coach and being restrained by our assistants. He was screaming in Albanian, but I knew his words were laced with foreign profanity. As I walked off the floor, a large coin ricocheted off the floor just inches from my foot. I avoided my usual reaction, which would be to angrily stare into the crowd to imply that I would kick the ever-living shit out of the culprit. Being that I was outnumbered, and my crazy paled in comparison to their crazy, I kept my head down and headed to the bench. Our coach made his way back to the huddle, still screaming, his face as red as the flairs glowing throughout the crowd. He told us to stay directly in front of the bench but on the court. Do not touch the ball, don't inbound the ball, basically, don't play basketball for the last seventeen seconds, and we will be champions, and we will be safe.

As we walked onto the court, the locker room doors swung open. Two lines of police officers in full riot gear quickly marched along the perimeter of the court in unison. It was like a scene out of *Game of Thrones* where the Unsullied created a protective barrier around Daenerys Targaryen. The police stopped and quickly turned to the crowd lifting their clear body-length shields on an angle above their heads. Peja inbounded the ball and quickly ran the length of the floor, and laid it in. We watched as the referee placed the ball on the ground, counted to five then called a violation. Peja quickly passed the ball in and scored again. Knowing that the game was already over, Peja took advantage of our coach's concern and scored four uncontested points. This made our fans irate. As the buzzer sounded, I heard another noise that piqued my attention. It was the sound of coins pelting off the wood floor. Our fans were firing coins at the Peja players and coaches for what they thought was a not classy move. Apparently, hurling small metal objects at an innocent human being is the best way to keep everyone classy. The Peja fans, not ones to be outdone by all the classiness, began hurling coins towards us.

The police force closed in around us with their shields still raised above their heads. We were ushered to the back wall below our bench and cocooned under the clear shields still being held high by the officers. The sounds of screaming fans, Albanian profanity, and metal coins bouncing off plastic shields were soon followed by the distinct sound of glass breaking. I was hoping it was Stone Cold Steve Austin sauntering down the aisle, ready to Stone Cold Stun the entire Peja crowd, but the sound was something far more ominous.

For some reason, the back wall of the balconies that housed the fan sections were lined with windows. This allowed for natural light, pleasant breezes, and, more importantly, small weaponized pieces of glass to use when you are pissed off that your team lost. The distinct sound of glass breaking was because the Peja fans were smashing those windows and hurling the dangerous shards at us. Let me clarify that a group of human beings who supported a basketball organization were punching through windows to break the glass, picking that sharp, dangerous glass up, and throwing it at a group of basketball players who were playing a game.

The seventeen of us sat, crouched down against the wall behind our bench surrounded by clear plastic shields, as the barrage of paraphernalia bounced off the clear force field. Every so often, a piece would make its way through our defenses. I heard a few teammates yell out in pain as the rest of us braced for impact. This onslaught continued for ten minutes or so until either they ran out of change, glass, or interest. The Peja fans slowly dispersed, and we were escorted to the middle of the floor to finally hoist the trophy over our heads. Only a handful of fans remained for the celebration; the rest presumably, headed outside to battle to the death for Albanian town pride.

Most games had some sort of pomp and circumstance from the spectators, whether the flares made their way onto the court or not. We finished that season with the treble, consisting of The Super League Title, The Kosovo Cup and the Kosovan Championship. Losing only two games, both of which came in the best of seven series final. Our fans called the three Americans into a meeting to discuss why we were tied at two games apiece to a lesser team. Two years earlier, I was sitting with the management group for the Cairns Taipans on the deck of an oceanside restaurant while they praised my efforts. Here, after losing only two games the entire season, I was sitting in an outdoor cafe, surrounded by the angry fan group, chain-smoking cigarettes, and passive-aggressively threatening my life.

"No more losses!" Ymer said as he pounded his hand on the table and walked away after a few minutes of scolding.

Brad, Keena and I looked at each other in horror. "Do you think they will kill us?" I asked.

Keena shrugged. "Screw it, let's win these next two games so we can get the hell out of here." Our mindset going forward was more than just winning but getting home as quickly as we could. The next two games were blowout wins, and we were crowned champions of Kosovo. We poured champagne, we drank from the trophy, and we partied like champions. Then after the hangovers wore off and we received our final paycheck, Keena, Brad and I hopped on a plane and got the hell out of there.

As we ascended above the clouds, I caught one more glimpse of the uneasy Kosovan terrain I had noticed on the flight into the land of strange events. The terrain was much like my experience, bumpy, uneasy, and oddly beautiful. Kosovo was intense. I spent about forty percent of my time there fearing for my life. But underneath the angry hooligans, who for some reason had a large stake in our team and the dilapidated buildings, there was a kindness and passion I had not seen in all my travels. The people of Kosovo had an excuse for being a little aggressive. They had fought hard for their freedom, freedom from the oppression that killed thousands of Albanians. I think I can forgive them for throwing a lit flare at my head.

Chapter 10

Winter Wonderland

Fun fact, when it is seven degrees Fahrenheit outside of a vehicle, but inside the car, your body generates enough heat to warm a small village, the evaporating moisture, with no escape, will create absurd amounts of condensation on the interior windows. Another fun fact, when that condensation inside your vehicle reaches absurdly cold temperatures because you live in the actual arctic, it turns to frost. It was a tidbit I learned first-hand during the final stop of my career in Tallinn, Estonia.

That year I found myself in the same situation I had dealt with the previous winter: waiting for a job. My career was progressing on a severe decline, and I was mentally struggling to maintain the professional basketball player work ethic needed while waiting for a job that may never come. Knee pain, declining talent and frustrations grew each day as I waited for my agent's number to flash across my flip phone. While this lapse in contractual basketball jobs was mentally debilitating, it did prompt my writing career.

I had heard about this new phenomenon sweeping the nation called blogging or yogging; it might be a soft "B." I decided to monitor my life as a stay-at-home athlete under the moniker *Waiting for Godunk*, a play on *Waiting For Godot*. It is a story about two men waiting for a man's arrival that would never come, similar to the contract I feared would also never come.

There had been some interest but nothing that materialized over the fall. A team in Syria offered me a contract. The Middle East has always been a scary proposition. Every nightmare scenario I had heard where a player's life was actually in danger occurred somewhere in that region. The absurd amounts of money offered in the area make the decision to risk your life for financial gain difficult. The contract in Syria did not offer very much money and considering it also contained some interesting death clauses, none of which listed Nazis, evil archeologists, or snakes. I passed. This was followed by a team in Turkey who had expressed interest as well. My agent Mike Siegel forwarded a message from the team representative with a provisional offer.

After quickly Googling what provisional meant, I decided to accept. The offer was not set in stone but handed out to multiple players. Whichever player they liked the most would get the contract, and the rest would end up exactly how I did. The offer had me leaving the following day with no itinerary, which gives you all the concrete information. I agreed, Mike passed along the information, and I went about packing my life to board a flight leaving in twelve hours. I carefully selected the items I would need over the next eight months and stuffed them in two suitcases and a carry-on. I had my flight number but not an actual ticket, which I figured would be resolved when I reached the airport. I loaded my suitcases into my truck, gave my dog a final pat goodbye and started the twenty-eight minute drive towards the airport.

It was around that time when the word *provisional* began swirling through my head. Every trip always started with an itinerary with definitive flight information. I stopped the car, called Mike, and asked for an itinerary from the team as the flight was scheduled to depart in three hours. Mike called me back before I made it to the Walt Whitman Bridge to tell me the *provisional* contract was sent to another player as well. He was in Greece at the time, a much cheaper travel option for the team, and *his* provisional offer became a formal contract. *My* provisional offer became $7.32 of wasted gas.

After spending the next three months substitute teaching, coaching basketball, writing and contemplating retirement, Estonia, more specifically, BC Kalev Cramo, decided to offer me a contract for the remainder of the season. My writing career had taken off during that time, with articles being featured on ESPN, Fox Sports, and my blog syndicated on SLAM Magazine Online and Hugging Harold Reynolds, which, I am certain, was part of the reason for the contract offer. BC Kalev Cramo was a top team in Estonia. They competed in the Estonian League, the Baltic League and the VTB United League, meaning taking a chance on a guy with a bad knee and three shortened seasons in three years seemed like a stretch, unless I could give them a little exposure. But I gave zero fucks as I wanted to see if I still had it. Spoiler alert, I did not.

I repacked understanding that I was going to an arctic climate in the middle of the winter. It did not take long to see precisely how arctic. Flying over the Gulf of Finland was the initial eye-opener. The large fifty-mile-wide body of water, which separates Finland and Estonia, was frozen solid. I had left an enormous snowstorm back in Philadelphia, but it was nothing like this. I deboarded the plane and quickly rooted through my bag in search of warmer clothes like the Jamaican Bobsled team in *Cool Runnings*.

I shuffled through the various clothes I jammed tightly into my bags for the journey. I grabbed one of the two sweatshirts I had packed hidden under all the stupid shit I brought. Like fancy clothes, flip flops, a Hawaiian shirt for some reason, along with the essentials like snow boots and a plethora of sweatpants and basketball gear as I ended up wearing the same thing every day.

Overseas basketball players will never make the GQ Style lists, as airline regulations prevent you from taking the entire contents of your wardrobe to a foreign destination. Even if they did, my wardrobe at the time was wildly dorky. Being that I was a professional basketball player and not a model yet, I figured I would be alright. I spent most of my Estonian days layered in team gear and a heavy jacket when I walked outside every morning to scrape the ice from both the interior and exterior of my car. As previously mentioned, the frost that accumulates on the outside of a car also accumulates on the interior during the frigid Estonian winters. Science is funny like that.

As I scraped the ice off the interior of my windshield in negative four-degrees, I reminded myself how much I loved the snow as an adolescent. Waking up to a field of fresh white powder outside my window, I would sit patiently in front of the radio, waiting for my school's number to be called to confirm a snow day. Hot chocolate with marshmallows was a staple drink during a winter school closure, along with building an enormous snowman in the front yard while putting the carrot in inappropriate spots. Then we would go sledding and Geoff threw caution to the wind and rocketed down a hill at 30 mph directly into a semi-frozen stream, causing the onsets of hypothermia, which, oddly enough, happened twice. In both instances, my mom quickly stripped him down to his underwear and wrapped him in a blanket in front of all our friends, first when he was six and again when he was ten. This occurred because one, my mom was more concerned about our safety than our feelings. And two, embarrassing the shit out of us was something my mom excelled at, like that cold February evening during my sophomore year in high school.

I had asked a senior named Becky Behen, who happened to be the hottest girl at Camden Catholic High School, to the Sophomore Cotillion. It was a real ballsy move on my part, as she was the epitome of a high school hottie: cute, athletic, popular and a body like the girls who graced the pages of *Playboy* magazine. I knew she was only going because my dorky friends asked her hot, cool friends and it would be a fun night out, but I still felt a sense of achievement. Despite my understanding that this date was strictly platonic, I was getting a vibe as the night went on. Now I was fifteen at the time and had no idea what a vibe even was, but something was telling me I may have a shot with her. She laughed at my jokes and smiled at me, things that pretty people do to people they like or people they feel bad for.

I was teetering on the holy shit she likes me/she wants nothing to do with me scale for most of the night, before an upperclassman walked up to us, looked at me, and said, "Maybe you will get lucky tonight."

My heart began racing. *Oh my god, this is so embarrassing! She is going to flat out reject me in five, four, three, two, one—*

"Maybe he will," she replied.

My heart, which was already beating at an unhealthy rate, went into official heart attack mode. *Is she joking?! I'm going to get lucky!? Me?!!* She turned and looked at me. "We are going to Mike Dennin's party after this, right?" It took all my power not to pass out. I began nodding my head up and down for an unnaturally long time.

After I did not dance, talk or breathe for the last forty-five minutes of the Cotillion, we made our way to the after-party. It was my first experience at a *cool kids* party, and I was doing everything I could to avoid embarrassment. I was sipping on a beer and talking with Becky when someone yelled out, "Where is Kevin Owens? His mom is on the phone."

I froze. *Oh my god, please tell me there is another Kevin Owens at this party!* I looked at Becky, horrified, and began to perspire. The emotional rollercoaster I had experienced in the last four hours was enough for an entire lifetime, and it was still nearing the final drop. I walked into the house, followed by the eyes of all the cool kids preparing mom jokes in their heads. I picked up the phone.

"Hello?"

My mother's distinct voice was on the other end, "Kevin, you have a curfew, and you never checked in. I had to call around for an hour to track you down. What the hell are you thinking? You need to be home in the next thirty minutes, or I am coming to pick you up!"

The phone clicked. I was left standing in Mike Dennin's kitchen, hoping a sinkhole would swallow me up. Becky walked up to me. "Everything ok?" she asked, as the combination of sweat and tears increased the moistness on my face.

"I think I have to go," I replied, fighting back the emotions that were building up inside.

"You have to go? Why? Is everything ok?"

"My mom gave me a curfew and is threatening to pick me up if I don't come home immediately."

Becky looked me in the eyes. "I wish you didn't have to leave," she said. There was a look in her eyes that made me think she might have wanted me to stay, but unfortunately, my mom was being a world-class cock-block.

I sat in silence, defeated as Becky drove me back to my house. The thought of trying to kiss this beautiful girl crossed my mind, adding another layer of apprehension to my already fragile state and causing my internal temperature to rise. To add another element of embarrassment, as my body heat rose, I began sweating profusely. It was hands down the most pressure-filled situation I had ever experienced, and I was blowing it.

I had been staring straight ahead, trying not to cry for most of the drive while the window condensation slowly surrounded me like an eerie fog. As we pulled up to my house, I glanced at Becky, who had a look of shock and disgust, noticing that half of her vehicle was completely obstructed by my science experiment going on in her passenger seat. Trying an awkward kiss at this point was outside any realm of possibility, as my embarrassment was at an unhealthy high, and the eventual rejection would have been life-altering. I looked up at her, panicked, said something along the lines of, "Thank you for being my date," hopped out, and quickly walked up the icy driveway. I walked up to my door and realized the extent of how poorly my body reacted to the intense situation I just endured. My shirt, which started off white, was clear.

After the experience in Becky's car, I never wanted to show my face at my high school, hometown or the state of New

Jersey ever again. I envisioned living in a cottage in Vermont far away from embarrassment, rejection and any sort of tropical climate. I pictured spending cold winter nights by a warm fire surrounded by enough Siberian Huskies to race the Iditarod.

Just like the car ride with Becky sixteen years earlier when the heat emulating from my body created condensation on the drive home and fogged up the windows, I again found myself in a similar situation. Only this time, the sweating was not because I was terrified of beautiful females, but because I had just endured the intense rigors of double session European practices. This led to me spending seventeen minutes each morning scraping and defrosting my car windows in the cold Estonian parking lot, somewhat relieved I never pulled the trigger on my Vermont dream. I would exit the car when I arrived at my apartment for the evening, and the dewy mist that gathered on the interior would freeze in the negative ten-degree night. I would walk out to the parking lot the following morning to find another seven to twelve inches of snow, a standard daily precipitation total, which I would brush off with my enormously long arms, then defrost, scrape, repeat.

It became my daily routine in Estonia: Wake up to a foot of snow, clear my car of the elements, put it in drive and reverse thirty to forty times until I finally broke through the snowdrift that blocked my exit, and then turn onto the main road, which was covered by ten inches of ice. I would then pull into practice, run sprints, sweat, leave practice, fog up my car, eat dinner and go to sleep. The routine was unwavering, that was until an Estonian magazine gave me a call.

I had written an article for the magazine, and they needed a face to put along with the words. Now, this wasn't my first modeling gig, as I had posed for basketball-related promotions before. There was the large cardboard cutout of myself in the local Kroger during my D-League days that tended to scare shoppers, sometimes even myself. A team photo in Cairns where I had to resemble a tough guy. And the fake ID photo I posed for in college under the alias Keith Ovens.

Fairly excited to throw down some *Estonian Blue Steel*, I agreed. Shortly after that, I received an email from the photographer telling me to be prepared for some light-hearted hijinks the following morning. I guessed since they wanted to play the funny angle, I should prepare for anything as having range is something only the top models possess. I had written about packing a pair of sandals during my trip to Estonia, and the photographer asked me to bring them along.

That night I ate a healthy meal, drank plenty of water, and attempted to get to bed early, so I would have a healthy glow come morning. I also loaded up on pushups and abs so my body would look good just in case they asked me to go shirtless, you know, typical model stuff. I toyed with the idea of finding a tanning salon to get some sun, as that particular star was absent in this Baltic country.

Unfortunately, that night was the worst night of sleep I had since I arrived. I awoke before dawn to my neighbors arguing. I can only assume this was a serious altercation, as yelling at that decibel at five-thirty in the morning does not scream a healthy relationship. I knew very little Estonian, but the word *sitapea* (asshole) was used often. I tried to ignore it and go back to sleep, however every ten minutes or so the arguing would pick up again, and some sort of object would be thrown against a wall. Eventually, the door slammed, and I was able to close my eyes. Then came the beeping. I did not know for sure what was happening outside besides the obvious snowfall. But one of the combatants had begun laying on the horn of their car. More screams from the balcony, more honking. Don't these people know I have a gig in the morning?

Eventually, the noise from outside subsided, and the beeping of my alarm clock replaced the car's horn. I sauntered out of bed, cursed myself for not buying cucumbers for my eyes, jumped in the shower, and was on my way to the photoshoot. When I arrived, I was met by the photographer who looked eerily excited. She informed me that we would be taking pictures in a snow-covered field just a few meters away. Oh, how fun, I thought as I scanned the room for a wardrobe.

"What exactly am I wearing today?" I asked.

"What you have on is fine," she said.

Is it? I arrived in my grey hooded sweatshirt, black sweatpants and snow boots. *Fucking amateurs!*

Dressed to the nines in my finest sweat clothing, we proceeded to the field. I noticed walking up to this snowy meadow that we were in uncharted territory. Neither human nor animal had ventured through this field in months. The large footsteps I was creating were the only of its kind. I also noticed the steps were getting deeper and deeper as the snow was getting higher and higher. I was soon about to find out why. The first pose was of me lying on the ground making a snow angel like a freaking child. I was not expecting hijinks of this magnitude when I took the gig, but I proceeded on. I took my first step onto this snowy terrain and immediately felt unstable. I could feel the three feet of packed snow beneath me, struggling to support my weight. My second step was equally horrible, taking my right foot a little deeper and nearly sending me tumbling. Then came the third step, which sent me plummeting through the snow. My left leg was now submerged up to my hip in the white abyss. In a foolish attempt to recover, I quickly jerked my left leg out, causing my right leg to suffer the same fate. As you can imagine, this sequence repeated itself several times until the photographer, safely on the solid ground fifteen feet back, told me to stop.

"Ok, turn and drop, then make a snow angel," she instructed. She began moving her hands up and down to her side as if I didn't go to Catholic school for twelve years and know what an angel looked like. As I turned, I began to think about the trust-building exercise I participated in when I was in second grade, in which I fell back into a group of peers whom I trusted to catch me. Although three of them still ate glue, I still trusted them more than I trusted the snow.

I closed my eyes, lifted my arms, and dropped, nearly disappearing in a snowy grave. I had fallen about a foot deep into the frigid frost.

"THAT'S PERFECT!" she yelled, the echoes eventually reaching me through the ice. "YOU CAN STAND UP NOW."

Can I? I began rolling myself out of the angelic hole and swam back to the photographer.

"Is that it?" I asked, covered in ice and snow and hoping for some relief to my now frostbitten toes. The snow had become wedged into my boots during my escapades across the field, and now my toes were freezing.

"Almost," she said, holding up the sandals.

Oh, what the hell? I began thinking of ways to tell my coach I could no longer play as four of my toes had to be amputated. I sat in the shallow snow and removed my boots and socks. The frigid air did not alleviate the stinging on my feet. She handed me the sandals and asked me to head back out to the deep end with nothing to protect my poor piggies.

If the one episode of *America's Next Top Model* I watched taught me anything, it's to be as sexy as I can despite any discomfort I may be feeling. I had to suck it up and give the people what they wanted. Although my bare feet were submerged in ice guarded only by a thin piece of rubber, I gave that camera the sexiest eyes I could and posed my ass off. My grey sweatshirt pictures with the ripped pocket and white flip-flops in the tundra came out as expected. I looked cold and uncomfortable, which was precisely what I was going for.

While my modeling and writing careers were flourishing, my basketball career was crashing to an end. I was a shell of my former self. The knee I injured in South Korea required 1200mg of ibuprofen every time I walked on the court. The pain medicine began fucking with the rest of my body, and my mind slowly realized this was it.

When I leave Estonia, I will never play another professional basketball game again. I always said I would play until it was no longer fun and no longer successful, and this was neither. I averaged a paltry 6.6 ppg, and while still led the team in rebounding, it was not enough to win any trophies for BC Kalev Cramo.

I took the court on March 28, 2010, for the last time as a professional athlete, winning the consolation series of the Estonian League. I ended my career with thirteen points and six rebounds during that game. As I walked off the court for the last time, a young fan walked up to me.

"Can I have your jersey?" he asked. Now, I had always taken my jerseys home with me to hang in a closet and occasionally stare at while reliving the glory days. This jersey was going to make a great addition to my living-in-the-past collection. I looked at this child who was staring up at me in awe. I thought about the impact this jersey may have on him, how I was still looked at as a celebrity, despite my frustrations.

"Sure, kid," I said to him with a smile. I took the jersey off, signed it and gave it to him.

He looked at me wide-eyed with a large smile across his face. "Thank you, thank you!" he repeated over and over.

I furrowed my brow while witnessing his reaction. In my mind, I was a failure. I did not achieve my dream of playing in the NBA. I had spent my career trying to reach the promised land and failed. No one knew who I was or how hard I worked. Like the walls of my high school gym, I was leaving this game without making a mark. I was not Michael Jordan or LeBron James. I was a nobody—a nobody in a snowy land thousands of miles away from my loved ones who could not even watch me play.

But something was different this day. On this day, in a small corner of the world, across the frozen fields and past the medieval walls that surrounded Tallinn, to this one young fan, I was a hero. I smiled back at him. "You got it, Bud. Take good care of it for me." He shook his head, and I gave him a high-five.

I turned and looked back at the court one last time. This large rectangle was the only constant I had in this ever-changing world. Each destination was different—different customs, different languages, different fans, different everything. But basketball never changed. It was still the same game I grew up playing in my driveway. It had taken me to four different continents, eighteen countries and forty-three American states and now it was taking me home for the final time.

Part 3

Overseas Nonsense

What All Overseas Athletes Have in Common

When I was a kid, I always wanted to fly. I looked at Superman, not as a fictional character with big muscles and great hair, but as a future career option. As a seven-year-old, that was my dream to fly around the world, helping people and wearing my underwear on the outside of my pants. It's ironic because I ABSOLUTELY HATE FLYING. Even though I love exploring the world, I find nothing positive about the experience until I have safely landed on the ground.

First, there is the issue of being a shade under 7-feet tall while planes are designed to accommodate anyone under 5-feet 2-inches comfortably. Apparently, when commercial airlines were a new and exciting venture, taller people did not exist. Or airlines thought of the grand idea to jam as many people as possible to maximize profits and minimize comfort. Regardless, being sardined into a small seat for a long trip is excruciating.

Next is the overall debilitating fear of air travel. It started on my high school senior class trip. At the time, I had zero fear of flying. The movie *Airplane* showed me that even an idiot could land a plane during an emergency. The flight from Philadelphia to Orlando was a breeze and, of course, incident-free. The trip went like every other senior class before me. Exploring Disney, posing for the pictures on Tower of Tower and getting drunk at Epcot as the middle-aged bartender in Germany thought I was hübscher (handsome). The flight back was the spark that ignited my anxiety. I sat next to a friend of mine who was petrified of flying. Our flight was bumpy, and every bit of turbulence caused her to sink slowly into madness. For those two hours, I held her hand, tried to make her laugh, all while her fears slowly rubbed off on me.

Little did I know her fear of flying would ultimately become mine. *If she was so worried, why wasn't I?* On the grand scale of life problems, fear of flying was way down on the list behind poor posture and hiding my boners, as I was not much of a frequent flyer at the time. It turns out being a college athlete, and then professional basketball player means spending most of the time in an airplane. And the more time you spend in the air, the more likely you are to experience all the things which could go wrong—things like unexpected drops or severe turbulence.

There was this one fun activity our pilot partook in where he tried to land three times only to nearly crash as our wheels came inches away from the ground along with our left-wing before the pilot launched us back into the air and the terrible storm. And finally, one adventure where we lost power to an engine on takeoff, causing the left side of the plane to dip violently before our pilot, or computer-generated flying program took over, leveled us off and flew us back to safety. These experiences caused me to question my mortality, pray and wonder how I would be remembered. Thankfully, each of these scenarios was met with relief when I reached the airport's interior alive, albeit severely traumatized. Although I was happy to be on the ground, the relief was short-lived, knowing that in just a few days, I would be jettisoned back into the atmosphere for more possible traumas and cramped spaces. This tiny fear often crept in my mind, even when I should have focused on my duties as a basketball player.

As my paranoia grew and started becoming a possible deterrent for my career, my physician finally prescribed a drug to help me cope with the frequent trips called Lorazepam. It's an anti-anxiety medicine that became my savior trapped in a fuselage 30,000 feet above the world. I was finally able to relax. That is, until random strangers who look at plane rides as an invitation to actively seek out new BFFs began constantly annoying me. Such was the case on the final plane ride of my career as I flew from Tallinn, Estonia, back to Philadelphia.

One of my many character flaws is a short-term memory loss, specifically when it comes to names. Long-term memory, I'm good. I can remember the name of the kid I sat next to in third-period physics my sophomore year—his name was Angel Lopez. But introduce yourself to me now, and a minute later, ask me to repeat your name, and I'll have no clue. It is nothing personal, just the way I'm wired.

I spent half that international flight speaking to a stranger whose name I will never know due to my short-term memory issues and because Lorazepam is pretty much like the Men in Black flashing that silver dildo in my face. From what I remembered of this conversation, the man had just begun some sort of job in international basketball scouting. I had just finished up an interesting and lengthy overseas career and had some knowledge to drop.

"So, could I consider you an expert?" he asked.

"Yeah, I think I'm an expert. Not to sound pompous, but I have experienced things very few people have. And for some reason, throughout my career, I have been a lightning rod for ridiculous situations."

"Oh, yeah? What kind of situations?"

As with most discussions I have had on overseas basketball, I shared my humorous anecdotes. Flares in Kosovo, snorkeling in Australia, the G-League, etc. The one specific discussion that I remember vividly during the nine hour flight was not about different stories from different lands but about how many athletes' experiences overseas are identical. While each country is unique, the stories shared amongst many of us in this fraternity are remarkably similar. Talk to any overseas basketball player, and they will all have matching tales. Stories about being paid, adjusting to the language, altering their playing style to conform with the specific country's playing style and dealing with the mental struggles that come when you are in a faraway land and, in most cases, all alone.

My single-serving friend had reminded me of those situations. I could have been any overseas basketball player speaking to him, and we could have had the same conversation. While there are so many things specific to different countries, many aspects of overseas basketball will always be the same.

Chapter 11

The Language Barrier

My second year in the D-League was an interesting one. I was one of three returning players from a roster of twelve. Twenty other players would join me in training camp, where I would again have to fight and scrap for a roster spot. One of the draftees was a young Korean man named Bang Sung Yoon. Bang, as we called him, spoke very little English and the remainder of us spoke absolutely zero Korean. Our interactions were limited to smiles and waves and pointing at random objects.

As luck would have it, Roanoke Dazzle's Head Coach Kent Davison appreciated my kindness and leadership skills. He asked if I would share an apartment with Bang to make sure he would be ok. I agreed, and the greatest sitcom scenario of all time played out. We would go to the grocery store, and Bang would point at products, and I'd put them in my cart. I would order his food at restaurants, and he would smile and give me a big thumbs up. We were the real-life, *Perfect Strangers*. Bang and I found ways to communicate with each other, and both his English and my Korean improved. I would hear him on his computer speaking to relatives so far away and thinking how difficult that must have been for him. Especially not knowing the language very well. Nothing prepares you for leaving your home country and being thrust into an entirely new culture.

As fate would have it, three years later, I would arrive in Korea, not knowing the language very well and adapting to an entirely new culture, while Bang's career had taken him back to his hometown, playing for the Seoul SK Knights. I was the one now smiling and giving gestures while my teammates helped me acclimate. I was the one Skyping home to my relatives at odd hours of the night. In most of the countries I visited, I knew I could find a few English-speaking folks; however, I felt like I needed a translator for my actual translator in Korea.

My translator, Lee, was probably in his early twenties, and I could not imagine he worked much in this field prior to my arrival. Lee spoke pretty good English but was not fluent in basketball. His English was very proper and would address my fellow import Keena Young and me like we were Noblemen instead of a couple of young basketball players. Keena and I would congratulate each other by calling ourselves *Beasts* or say things like *That's dope,* and Lee would think we were insulting each other. He was confused as to why we would yell *Beast Mode,* assuming that there was a large predatory animal nearby.

During one timeout, my coach was yelling and cursing at me in Korean. Again this was a common occurrence, and Lee attempted to perform his duties. Before I continue, I should tell you that despite the broken English, Lee didn't seem to grasp basketball concepts. He would use phrases like "Pass the ball down to the other player and then sprint to that line where another player will divide you from your defender. Then turn to receive the ball and perform a shot jump."

Umm…what? In retrospect, it seemed like a very roundabout way to describe a simple screen.

So, during this one timeout, my coach was attempting to tell me that I needed to rebound better in his native tongue; at least, I think that's what he was saying. Our bench was located directly in front of a loud crowd, which drowned out his instructions. My coach was yelling something along the lines of, (this is my attempt at writing the sound I heard) "HAWSINGWAAAAAA."

I looked to my translator, who apparently also had a hard time hearing. Again, "HAWSINGWAAAAAA".

The seconds were rapidly ticking away in this timeout, and all I was hearing was HAWSINGWAAAAAA. This time my translator, still unaware of what was being said, decided to adlib. "Put the opposing player out further."

Not knowing what matter of the game he was referring to, I yelled out, "What?" My coach, infuriated at this point, threw out a few words I recognized as swears. My response was simple, efficient, and to the point, "What?" At this point, the lid was officially blown off the situation. The coach was livid. We were in a tense situation, and the most important player in the transpiring play was staring blankly at him.

Lee stood next to me on the sidelines repeating the phrase "PUT THE OPPOSING PLAYER OUT FURTHER!!" He kept getting closer and closer to my ear, thinking it was a noise issue and not a *what the fuck are you talking about* issue.

My coach was glaring at me like I just pushed over his mother. The one English word I knew he could say was "Kevin." He shouted my name, looked me in the eyes, like I was the one messing up this interaction, and screamed, "Kevin....HAWSINGWAAAAAA!"

Holy shit! "Lee, why would I push my man out further? We are on offense."

"Because he is too close to the backboard." *What the actual fuck is happening right now?* Eventually, I just shook my head in agreement and took the court.

I took the ball that possession, faced my defender up, drove hard with my right hand, and shot an actual reverse layup, and scored. I looked over at Lee, who gave me a thumbs-up, like me breaking off the play, and going one on one was exactly how we drew it up. Still to this day, I am not sure what transpired or what was trying to be conveyed. I took from this experience how much of a problem a language barrier can be playing overseas.

Korea was especially difficult due to the complexities of the language and the fact that very few people spoke English, or at least that is what I thought. After being released by Mobis Phoebus, my coach pulled me aside and spoke to me in perfect English, telling me he appreciated me. Though a few days before, he was threatening my well-being. Apparently, he spends the off-season in California with his family. I guess he wanted to keep the imports in the dark so they wouldn't see him as a kind human being.

Talking to referees overseas also presented a new challenge. It's an experience I would compare to raising a puppy. An animal has no idea what the hell you are saying 99% of the time. "Please, Please, PLEASE stop pooping all over the floor," as the dog tilts their head, looks right at you and poops on the floor. Trying to speak to referees in non-English speaking countries is a lot like that.

"How is that a foul," I would scream. The ref, not even making eye contact, would keep running past me like it was a rhetorical question. But the few words they understood were the words gentlemen like myself shouldn't be using.

Playing in South Korea was my first experience in a non-English speaking country. I, as expected, became engulfed in foul trouble quite quickly. I was pissed and confrontational, thinking I could get away with a blatant curse off of an official. I threw the always classy phrase, "You Don't Know Shit!" The referee, who had ignored every one of my pleas for mercy prior, perked his ears up with that last phrase.

"I DON'T KNOW SHIT?" he screamed in a Korean accent.

Oh shit, he can hear me. The referee walked up to the scorer's table and told them something; my coach then looked at me and started yelling and cursing at me again in Korean. It was quite a chaotic moment, all caused by my testing of the vernacular. Unfortunately, in my enraged state, I didn't realize that these refs had heard every American curse word by now. As expected, I was not rewarded for my poor choice of words and was, as my translator would later tell me, awarded a warning for cursing.

Other non-English speaking countries had less of an issue with communication. Coaches and team staff spoke primarily English to the Americans, a product of having new imports every year and needing those imports to be the offense's focal point. On the court, there were very few issues. Off the court, however, was a completely different story. Being in a foreign land with no ability to communicate or any sense of where you are can be a scary thing.

Let me preface by saying, I think it is ignorant for Americans to go overseas and assume that everyone will accommodate their cultures and language. I made a point of trying to assimilate myself into their environment. I adapted to their customs and culture the best I could while trying my best to learn their language. Although, sometimes, learning all this information in just a few days is impossible.

I had just gone to Barnes and Noble and purchased Complete Swedish, *The Ultimate Guide to Understand the Swedish Language*, a ritual I performed before leaving on any globetrotting assignment. The contract for the Swedish team was being faxed over to my agent's office, and I would be putting pen to paper within the next few hours. I had a week before I was scheduled to leave, allowing me some time to learn some simple Swedish words.

"Hej, Talar nagon har engelska?" I repeated aloud. My go-to phrase when traveling abroad, translated to, "Hello, do you speak English?" I was working through the pronunciations when my phone rang. My agent seemed annoyed. "Hey, Mike, what's up?"

Mike went on to tell me that the contract had not been faxed over, and he was losing patience, as this was our second day of waiting. "Another job just came across for you if you are interested. It is a better team, more money, but…"

"But what?"

"Well, it is in Kosovo, and you need to leave tomorrow."

I am ashamed to admit that I had no idea where Kosovo was located. During my early teens, I knew who President Bill Clinton was for two reasons: he allegedly received a blow job in the Oval Office and one of his lesser-known accomplishments, liberating the Kosovaran people from the Serbians. Statues of Clinton were spread throughout the country as a symbol of his importance. The historical significance of these events was lost on a young boy trying to imagine, first, what a blow job was, and why people would be mad that he received one.

I was forced into a tough decision, leave immediately for a country that had been a warzone two decades ago for more money, or wait on the possibility of a Swedish team sending a contract, which could wind up being bullshit. I went for the secured money and the uncertain republic. I informed Mike and immediately began packing for my next venture, on a flight leaving in just eighteen hours. Lost in the shuffle was another trip to Barnes & Noble to grab a different book on how to speak, whatever they spoke in Kosovo. I arrived in Prishtina speaking absolutely zero Albanian. There were not any books at the airport to help me with the language barrier I was soon set to face.

Usually, when I arrive at a new destination, I write down my address just in case, for some reason, I'm separated from familiarity I have a way to communicate where I lived. It was 2009, and a phone was used for calls, texts and the occasional game of Snake.

On the first week of my arrival, my teammates introduced me to the Albanian burek or, as they called it, *pite*. This flaky dough filled with sausage became the norm for my breakfast routine. I would go to a small restaurant below my apartment building and talk to Ajola, who spoke very little English, but appreciated my commerce and would hug me when I arrived each morning.

One morning I woke up starving as usual and made my way to Ajola's spot for some burek. The door was locked, and a note, written in Albanian, was taped to the front door. As previously mentioned, I do not speak nor understand Albanian. Trying to decipher why the restaurant was closed and where Ajola had gone was impossible, especially with the utter starvation I was experiencing. My teammates had told me the best food was located on Raki Street, a popular part of Prishtina. Hunger clouded my judgment as I waved down a cab and simply said Raki Street. The cab driver spoke little English and told me that the best burek was located elsewhere. "I take you fifteen minutes, no problem." I simply nodded, as any more movement would have eaten away at the four remaining calories I had in my body.

Now I had been in Prishtina for a little over a week and was still getting used to the nuances of my surroundings. The cab driver was taking me to a more unfamiliar area than the unfamiliar area I already was not familiar with. These thoughts usually run through my logical mind when I am in a normal mental state, but I wasn't in a normal mental state. I was overcome by hunger from the nearly fifteen hours since I last ate and the caloric burning that occurs from the vigorous physical activity of a professional basketball player.

If we are being honest with each other, there were probably five to six occasions in Kosovo that I gave myself fifty-fifty odds I would be robbed, murdered and cut up into more manageable pieces. As we drove further and further away and the wispy-haired driver continuously turned around and smiled, this became one of the times I saw my life flash before my eyes.

I was in a near-catatonic state when we pulled up to the make-shift restaurant that looked more like a cafeteria with long wooden tables and a group of people cutting up the long, delicious sticks of the burek. Stepping out of the cab, I turned to the driver to ask if he could wait for me since he knew where he had picked me up. By the time I opened the restaurant door and turned to make sure he was still there, all that was left was the cloud of exhaust. I took my place in the burek line.

Like Chipotle, one woman stood taking orders while the rest of the staff quickly chopped up the different pastries and put them on a tray as you moved along the glass partition quickly, paying at the end.

Finally, it was my turn. I had a toxic combination of hunger and anxiety, overtaking me as I stepped up to order.

"Çfarë doni?" the lady asked as I stared blankly at her. I smiled a big smile, thinking if she thought I was nice, she would understand I was an ignorant foreigner and just pass me my breakfast.

"Burek," I replied.

"Doni të keni një të ëmbël? Ose do të donit mish, vezë dhe spinaq?" she asked.

Here we go again. I stared at her, smiled and repeated, "Burek."

"Shkoj!" she shouted at me, waving her hand and shooing me down the line. The smile did not work as I had anticipated.

After what felt like an hour, the lunch lady slapped five large pieces of burek on the tray and shooed me along. The cashier must have witnessed my chaotic trip through the line. Not allowing me to make any more of a mockery, she shouted in broken English,

"Seventeen euro! You understand?"

I stood holding the money in my hand like Keanu Reeves' character Marlon James in the 1990 movie *I Love You to Death*, another R-rated title I probably should not have been watching at ten years old. The angry lady snatched a 20 euro from my hand and dropped a few coins in return. I tried the smile again, and she shot me a face of pure disgust. Apparently, all the smiles in the world were not helping me win these people over. I took my tray and sat down to devour my expensive breakfast.

My hunger fog was lifted, and I began to have logical thoughts again. I realized I had absolutely no fucking idea where I was, and worse, had no idea how to get to where I was going. I began thinking of landmarks to describe to any English-speaking cab drivers I could find. I knew there was some sort of large monument with a phrase on it directly in front of the gym, but I had never stopped to read it. If I could get there, I would be fine.

I walked to the road and began waving down anyone willing to take me back to familiarity.

An older man pulled up, with dimmed large bifocals, wearing a cloth vest, dress shirt and a white tight bullet-shaped hat that sort of made his head resemble a penis. I explained my situation to him, hoping he spoke enough English to figure out where I was. He smiled blankly at me, pointed to the restaurant I stood in front of, and gave me an ok sign, along with a gesture in which he faked eating. I knew that he could not understand me. But like me, just a few moments earlier in the burek line, he kept smiling. I repeated the phrase "Sigal Prishtina" over and over again, hoping that he knew the location of our games and could drive me there. He smiled and held up his hand as though he understood me and then proceeded to dribble an imaginary ball.

"Yes!" I exclaimed. "Basketball, Sigal Prishtina," and I got into the car.

He turned to me and smiled. "Where to?" he inquired.

"Sigal Prishtina," I responded.

His smile, which was so infectious that I too smiled from ear to ear, slowly went from nice to confused. I could tell he was not grasping what I was trying to tell him. I tried to figure out how to describe the large monument consisting of an English saying, but I could not remember the word which created it. We stared at each other for another minute or so before I decided to exit the vehicle, thinking I had a better shot with a different navigator.

The driver frantically rolled his window down and yelled, "Wait, ju lutem!" He began pointing at his cellphone. "Wait, wait...call." He scrolled through his phone then held it to his ear. "English. English," he told me, pointing to his phone and handing it to me.

"Hello," I spoke gently into the small cell phone.

"Where you go?" a deep voice answered me in barely decipherable English. It occurred to me that he had phoned an English-speaking friend to act as some sort of a cellular translator.

"So I need to get to Sigal Prishtina's arena for practice, which starts in thirty-five minutes," I told him. His response was the opposite of what I hoped for.

"Where?"

Frustrated, I explained to him that I do not know where it is, thus why I was speaking to him and not driving to practice with his friend. I attempted to explain the monument to him, to which he replied, "Yes, I know of monument, which one?"

This conversation was not going well. I handed the phone back to the driver, shook my head and walked away. As I hurried towards a more populated area, thinking the more people, the more likely to find someone who spoke English, I came face to face with a poster showing Kosovo's beauty. Among the seven pictures on the small billboard was the unmistakable sight of the familiar statue. It was the monument!

"N-E-W-B-O-R-N, NEWBORN," I shouted in euphoria.

I turned to see the cab driver still sitting in his car. I ran towards him frantically, waving my hands. "STOP!" I yelled as he nearly finished rolling his window up. "NEWBORN!" I yelled. "The monument, it says NEWBORN!" The driver looked at me with his familiar confused smile, immediately informing me that again, he had no idea what I was talking about. "Your phone!" I told him, pointing to the cell phone I just used. He picked it up and handed it to me. "No, you have to call your friend again!"

I ripped the phone from his hand and hit the TALK button, assuming he did not call anyone in the short time since our last call. I recognized the voice on the other end and yelled into the phone, "NEWBORN MONUMENT!"

There was a long pause. I thought the call was disconnected, and I nearly hung up before the voice responded, "Yes, Newborn Monument."

"Can you get me there?" I asked him.

"Yes, where are you located?" he replied. *You have to be goddamn kidding me right now!* I tried not to smash the phone on the ground and start sprinting to practice, which now started in just twenty-eight minutes. I took a deep breath, handed the phone back to the driver, and pointed to the receiver and then my ear.

The smile which had momentarily left his face slowly reformed, which meant that my smile, which was nonexistent, crept back across my face. *I was saved!* The old man nodded his head and kept repeating the word "Po," which I knew to mean yes. He waved to me in jubilation, and I lept back into the vehicle. I pointed to my wrist to indicate the little time we had to get me to that monument. "Ok!" he yelled as we whipped around the city. The fear of reaching practice alive overshadowed my fear of being late and fined by the team. Apparently, traffic laws are not as important in Kosovo as in America. We ran a total of three red lights, all of them directly in front of a police car, which glanced up and went about their business.

The smiling elderly man I first met was now an aggressive driving machine hell-bent on collecting his fare. We screeched to a stop, and he held his hand out the window, emphatically pointing. All my excitement slipped away into a large pit in my stomach as I sadly stared at a large statue of Bill Clinton waving. I was doomed. Yes, it was a monument, yes it represented the birth of Kosovo as a nation, and yes, I glanced at the metal crotch for some reason, since by that point I had an understanding of what a blow job was, and I realized Clinton had some brass stones.

I officially had only ten minutes until practice began, and I still did not know where I was. Then out of the corner of my eye, I saw it. In the distance, a familiar pointed set of towers rose from the buildings below. *There is the gym!* I grabbed onto the driver's shoulders and pointed in the direction. Like Vin Diesel's character, Dominic Toretto, he shoved the car into drive, slammed on the gas and headed towards the high curved towers. Seven minutes remained as we pulled up in front of the gym. I did not know how to end this relationship. It was the deepest relationship I ever formed with someone who could not understand a single word I spoke. We were now forever bonded by my love for the burek, utter starvation and lack of common sense.

I tossed him thirty euros, gave him one last smile, and sprinted into the gym, lacing my shoes up just as we began stretching. I made it. I had navigated the unforgiving streets of a foreign country with no knowledge of my whereabouts and no understanding of the language. This, however, is a cautionary tale. I spent forty euros on breakfast, and it nearly cost me a lot more than that.

Moral of the story: if you are in a foreign place, make sure you know where you are going. If you find yourself randomly looking for an adventure and decide that wandering around Kosovo would be a thrill, don't be a hero; learn the language first.

I learned my lesson that day. I now proceed with caution when traveling in a foreign-speaking land. Australia and New Zealand were easy since they spoke English, at least it sounded like English. They did speak the same language, and most of the time, I could understand the words they were saying, but just not why they were saying those words in that part of the sentence. Like when I was asked if I wanted to go to McDonald's with the phrase, "Makin' a Macca's run?" Which had my Australian roommate on the road respond with, "Let me slap on my thongs (flip flops), and I'll come with."

Other times, however, I could not understand a single thing they said. "A few roos loose in the top paddock" meant you were crazy, which I was called after destroying my towel on national television. "Your shout on the bevys, KO," which meant I was up to buy a round of drinks. Aussies also abbreviate everything and usually put a "Y" at the end of all these abbreviations. Brekky is short for breakfast, choccy is short for chocolate and biccy is short for biscuit or cookie. So, asking for a chocolate cookie for breakfast will take you under two seconds.

New Zealand had similar phrases, but those phrases were more difficult to understand due to the fast nature of their dialect. After spending a year in Australia, I was familiar enough that it was not a culture shock for me. The only issue I had was the first time someone called me *Bro*. Now this word in New Zealand is like saying "Hey, Man" in America. "How is it, Bro" pronounced,

"Ho iz eet brew" is considered a normal greeting and socially acceptable. Again, I did not read the manual before arriving and had a run-in on my first week.

In America, calling someone *Bro* is not a compliment. It can be offensive. After practice one day, I thought I pushed the button for the elevator in my apartment building, but it never illuminated. A kind gentleman pushed it again, smiled, and said, "Easy as, Bro." I took offense to his wording and assumed he was calling me stupid.

"Who are you calling, Bro?" I said, turning menacingly.

"Easy, Bro, we're good as gold," he replied, putting his hands up defensively. I could tell he did not have any aggression and seemed confused by my anger. Trying to save face, I quickly turned around and stood in awkward, embarrassing silence for the next forty-five seconds until I reached my floor.

One of my biggest regrets during the nine-year circus was not becoming fluent in a foreign language. I've had several teammates who spoke multiple languages, and I wondered in amazement about what logistical techniques went into switching effortlessly from one language to another. I tried to learn basic phrases, which I intended on building upon, but when the rest of the team and coaching staff spoke English, I usually slacked on my Rosetta Stone. Because of that slacking, my dialect consists of just a few foreign curse words, a couple of everyday phrases, and pretty wicked Australian, New Zealand and Eastern European accents. While I did not always learn every aspect of the language, which in turn brought me seconds from disaster, I did try. In a foreign land, respect and effort will take you a long way. And if all else fails, just smile.

Chapter 12

Adaptability

Up until 2011, I lived my life by the sound of the whistle. The high-pitched blow meant only two things: I was right, or possibly I was wrong. For that split second, a gut-wrenching feeling would overcome me. It lingered as the ref walked to the scorer's table and held up my number with his fingers. To this day, that high-pitched sound transports me back in time.

When I was sixteen, I was asked to referee a night of middle school summer league basketball. Since I played the game my entire life, I felt confident in my basketball knowledge and ability to display it out on the court. My coach had insisted on me refereeing, offering me $10 a game, which to a sixteen-year-old was an exorbitant amount of money. Remember, this was 1996, and $30 could buy about sixty beers and a bottle of Aftershock. Not that I was a crazy kid who would constantly go out drinking, but peer pressure is a bitch, and there was a girl named Katie Zobel I was trying to impress. She had decided to come and watch me referee, knowing that after the game, we would hang out, and I would possibly be able to get her beer, and she would possibly be able to touch my leg. This was one of only a few perks of dating me during my adolescence, as I was a gangly awkward kid, but being that I was so tall, I was able to confuse the cashiers at the local liquor stores.

It created a new and more nerve-wracking opportunity for me. Although my face looked twelve, my body was larger than most adults. Because of my superior height, I was constantly designated to buy beer for my friends, an experience that was both terrifying and exhilarating. If ever Hollywood pinpointed the exact feeling of a situation, it was in the movie *Superbad*. The rollercoaster of emotions that takes place when you are an underage high school student trying to buy alcohol is unmatched.

I would act super confident when they asked me to buy the beer, trying to maintain the role of cool leader. Deep down, my mind suffered from the sheer panic that I would be arrested or, worse, killed for trying to get alcohol while underage. The fears were nearly debilitating as I walked up to the counter, trying to maintain what little confidence I had.

When successful, pure euphoria replaced the fear as I tried to hide the enormous smile from the cashier while saying something super adult-like such as, "I guess we don't have to worry about that Unabomber guy anymore, huh?" The cashier, who obviously didn't give a shit before, would suspiciously look at me as I quickly walked to my car and sped off. I became a conquering hero to a group of high school students, and the cute girl named Katie, who decided she wanted to hang out with me that night.

Katie was waiting for me in the parking lot as I pulled up to the Atlantic Avenue outdoor courts in Haddon Heights, New Jersey, fifteen minutes before tipoff. My grade school coach, Tim Lenahan, met me at the scores table and walked me over to the league's director and proprietor of the greatest and most unfortunate name of all time, Kenny Hamburger. Kenny handed me a whistle and a black and white striped shirt and went over the league's rules, like a running clock and one point and one foul shot on all shooting fouls.

With Katie in the crowd and because I was sixteen years old, I decided I would play this whole referee thing super cool.

That meant not running up and down the court and making eyes at her anytime a kid missed a shot or fell, holding back my laughter. In the first few minutes of the period, my lackadaisical approach was met with giggles from Katie and building frustration from the parents in the crowd.

"Hey, Hamburger!" one parent yelled, "We are not paying you to have some kid ref this game!"

Being the people pleaser that I was, I felt an instant sense of embarrassment. I also realized that Kenny would find someone else to ref the final two games if I did not give more effort, and I'd be out $20 worth of beer money and the possible admiration of my crush sitting courtside.

I stepped up my game, blowing the whistle more often and getting myself in a better position to make calls. The damage, however, was already done. The parents had made up their mind that I was a bum and that I didn't care, despite my change in attitude and effort. One dad was especially rotten, pointing out any touch, push or sneeze I may have missed. He did this indirectly, which made it even worse. "Hey, Hamburger, that's not a foul?!"

Only Kenny was not the one refereeing. I was. My confidence drained from my body with each tick of the clock. As luck would have it, this game came down to the wire, the absolute worst situation to be in if you are an unconfident referee being heckled by a dad, hellbent on being a cock-block that evening. It was a tie game with just eight seconds remaining, and the yellow team, consisting of one extremely large boy who scored eighty-five percent of their points, had the ball on the sideline. His team inbounded the ball and immediately threw it to this adolescently enhanced kid in the low post. The large boy took one dribble, turned and dropped his shoulder hard into the sternum of the skinny undersized kid trying to guard him. The poor defender fell hard to the pavement while the large brute laid the ball in for the winning basket. I froze. I knew it was an offensive foul, but I was unsure if that were a call I could make with just three seconds remaining.

A faint sound came from my whistle as the ball dropped through, surprising everyone in attendance, most of all me. *Oh shit*, I thought as all eyes turned to me, unsure if that was a whistle or a bird chirping in the trees. My eyes widened as I tried to decide what to do. I had to call something. If I called a foul on the poor skinny kid who just was railroaded, the large boy would shoot an extra free throw, and the game would be over, ending this misery. If I called a charge, the parents of the yellow team would most likely erupt, light their torches and carry me away to my doom. Seconds were passing as I told myself to do something, anything, anything at all!

My left hand instinctively grabbed onto the back of my head, and I took my right hand and stretched it out, pointing towards the opposite end of the court. I had done it. I had called a charge!

"ARE YOU KIDDING ME, KID?" the heckler screamed. Apparently, the large child was his son, and he could not believe I had the audacity to call a foul on his soon-to-be NBA All-Star son. He walked onto the court and called me a joke before being restrained by my grade school coach. Reminder, I was sixteen years old, extremely skinny, and looked like a little kid to anyone but the cashiers of all liquor stores.

Kenny raced to my aid and told the guy to leave. "C'mon, Tony," the angry parent yelled to his son. Tony gave me an equally disgusted look as he walked by. I stared back at him with similar disdain.

"Enjoy the peak of your basketball career now," I whispered under my breath as Tony's dad was about 5-feet 8-inches tall and shaped like a melon. Without enormous Tony taking up the entire lane, the green team came down in sudden death overtime and scored easily, winning the game and initiating me into a fraternity of a group I would come to despise.

Being a professional basketball player means having to learn how to deal with referees appropriately. And having to deal with referees who enforce a different set of rules specific to that particular country makes adhering to the rules a far more difficult task. Each country has its own distinct definition for the word foul. Had I played my whole career in one league with one specific set of expectations, I would have been able to anticipate the general flow of the game. I would have known how aggressive I could or could not have been. The subtle differences between each league make adjusting to each new situation that much more stressful.

In New Zealand, while I adjusted quickly to life off the court, I quickly learned that referees were more lenient with the whistle than in my past experiences. I learned this lesson first hand after being punched directly in my face in front of a referee. He did nothing. There wasn't even so much as a stoppage of play. I shoved the guy back. He tumbled to the floor and tried to trip me as I ran past. I kicked his leg away and the ref yelled "Easy, Fellas, eaaaaasssssssy. Don't make me get involved." We played on. Most nights I wasn't sure if I was playing basketball or rugby. I learned to adjust to the physicality of the league, toughening me up a bit and allowing me to lead the league in rebounding.

The following season I had to readjust my aggressiveness completely. European basketball had a different style and very limited patience for fouling. Basketball was viewed as a beautiful dance, not a barbaric melee. Because of this philosophy, physicality was prohibited. People with restraining orders were allowed more contact than I was. Had the incident from the previous year occurred, I would have most likely been arrested. It all depends on the style of basketball in that specific location, which made adjusting to these new rules each year quite stressful.

While referees generated most of my rage, they became just one of the many variables that made playing overseas basketball unique. As previously mentioned, overseas contracts change every year. One season you are making six figures and flying on private planes; the next season, you're making far less and sitting next to an overweight man who keeps battling for an armrest in coach. Every season brings a new locale, a new lifestyle and a new set of rules.

My initiation into the subtle basketball rule differences came during my first full year abroad in Cairns, Australia. My assistant coach, Aaron Fearne, was a native Kiwi (New Zealander) but played collegiately in the United States. He had a good feel for basketball rules I was used to but knew what I could get away with abroad. He opened my eyes to the new style of play, showing me what was not considered a travel in Australia. A traveling violation occurs when a player takes multiple steps without dribbling the ball. If that planted pivot foot lifts up, referees are instructed to immediately call a travel violation. My non-pivot foot can dance an Irish Jig, just as long as my other foot was planted firmly on the ground.

Fearne taught me that when I had established and planted my one foot after my two free steps, in Australia, it was legal to lift my pivot foot and take the third step past the defender creating space and enabling me to lay the ball into the basket. This move is similar to the wildly popular Euro step, which allows the offensive player an extra half step to gain an advantage and fool the defender who still believes the game is being played under the standard set of rules.

This new move became part of my post routine from that point on. I would use it throughout my travels; it was usually successful and never ended with a traveling violation. That is until a summer league game during one of my brief stops home. The Delco Pro Am was a summer league consisting of NBA, overseas and high-level college basketball players from the Philadelphia area. The competition was fierce, allowing me a chance to compete against pro athletes during the short overseas offseason.

It was the semifinals of the Delco Pro Am, and my team, consisting of my brother, me and some University of Pennsylvania alumni, matched up against 76ers star Lou Williams and several tough interior defenders. It was well into the second half, and all my run-of-the-mill North American moves had thus far been unsuccessful. I figured it was time to break out some international flavor. I caught the ball on the post, took one dribble to the baseline, and gave a little Dream Shake, a move made popular by Hall of Famer Hakeem Olajuwon. The defender stayed squarely behind me as I turned over my right shoulder to shoot a jump shot. This clever brute crowded my right hand as I attempted to throw a shot fake.

Unfortunately, he did not bite; instead, he remained stuck to my right side. It was Euro step time. I faced the basket, stepped by him with my left foot, then lifted my pivot foot and glided by him to the basket. I could hear him mutter, "What the fuck?" as I laid the ball into the basket. The other eight players stopped and stared in confusion, not really sure why I had just taken four steps with only one dribble. The only person not confused by my epic footwork was the referee standing at the baseline, who immediately called a travel and yelled to me, "This ain't Europe."

I ran back on defense, trying to explain myself to my teammates, who just rolled their eyes and told me to find my man. This was just one example of the many subtle differences between the American game and the international game.

The different rules were not just limited to on-court but off-the-court situations as well. Two of the strangest rules I encountered were introduced to me during my tryout for the KBL in Las Vegas. During the testing portion of the combine, we were shuffled through lines and asked to do random tasks like jumping, squatting and standing straight while they measured our official height and weight. Unbeknownst to me at the time, the KBL had a height restriction. Both imports could not be over thirteen-feet two-inches combined. And no one player could be over 6-feet 8-inches. Being that I had been listed anywhere from 6-feet 9-inches to 7-feet tall, I knew this was trouble. It was like when Geoff and I had to take the walk of shame after trying unsuccessfully to cram our enormous bodies into the new Batman and Robin ride at Six Flags. While the outcome of being too tall for this experience could be financially devastating, at least it wouldn't have been life-threatening.

I was not privy to this odd Korean Basketball League rule until fellow Philadelphian Reggie Osaka, who I spent my summers working out with, turned to me and whispered, "Don't make yourself six-feet ten-inches. Make yourself smaller."

"Why?" I asked.

"They will kick you out if you are taller than six-eight."

I was only seven players away from the height taker and had just received a truth bomb. I was terrified. I had traveled cross country for this opportunity, and my stupid tall head was going to cost me hundreds of thousands of dollars. As I slowly crept towards the measuring station, I was sweating like a drug mule waiting to go through customs. I have always had a slight hunch in my posture. People constantly told me to stand up straight and don't slouch. What they didn't understand was that all things were taking place underneath me: my friendships, my crushes and my daily chores, all interacting and existing ten inches below my eye level.

I had spent years constantly looking down at everyone while also trying not to stand out in the crowd. *Wait a minute. I have been practicing for this moment my entire life. This embarrassing lack of posture was going to be my ticket to fortune.* I reached the front of the line and stepped to the measuring man.

"Stand up straight" he snipped at me. I tugged my shorts low, slightly bent my knees and assumed my normal slouched head position. "STRAIGHT!" he yelled.

I kept my neck hunched but tilted my head back. He was so very small, and I was so very tall that he did not notice my hunch, probably assuming that was how God made me. "Six-eight," he yelled to the registrar. I pumped my fist as I walked to the next station, knowing I had successfully navigated a way around the strangest rule I would ever encounter. Well, one of the strangest.

Korea had another extremely odd rule. Imports were only allowed to play together during the first and fourth quarters. Which meant during the second and third quarters, either me or my teammate Keena Young would sit on the bench. It was an extremely bizarre rule that was in place to give the native-born Korean players more playing time. I was unaware at the time that

I would be traveling to the other side of the earth only to play half a game. This rule allowed our coach to pick whichever one of us was playing better at the time, which usually ended up being Keena. I would head to the bench and watch the fans bang pieces of plastic together instead of cheering and watching our two trainers stumble around like buffoons anytime someone incurred an injury that often happened because of our rigorous schedule.

This became another issue with the subtle differences from country to country. Some organizations like Mobis worked players to exhaustion, never allowing rest and creating situations where they were more susceptible to injuries. It would lead to one of the scarier aspects of overseas basketball. Trusting your health and, in some cases, life to a team trainer you have never met, who doesn't speak your language and have no knowledge of their qualifications or credentials.

In normal circumstances, we end up trusting doctors we don't know during emergencies. This is easier to do in your native land. There is more trust that the men and women taking care of you spent their collegiate experience studying and not lighting a throwing hammer on fire and launching it into a tree, like my college roommates. Most people do not research the qualifications of medical professionals outside the United States, and I was no different. I had hoped that if something went wrong, I could trust the professionals who were hired to keep me safe. That wasn't always the case. Emergencies happen no matter where you are or what you do. Emergencies tend to happen more frequently when you are a professional basketball player.

I've had quite a few emergencies in my career, including a severe asthma attack caused by a dusty cold arena the day after a country concert causing me to collapse on the court and be rushed to the hospital, scaring the shit out of my teammates and coaches. I experienced a concussion from an errant opponent's finger being jammed into my eye socket, causing my eye to temporarily pop out of place, which is why I still wear glasses to this day. However, these cases took place in Roanoke, allowing me access to medical personnel I trusted. Being injured overseas was a completely different story. You only could hope that the people paid to protect you would do just that. You also hoped that their medical certifications did not come from the back of a cereal box. I am still not totally convinced was the case in South Korea when I had two jackasses misdiagnosing my knee, causing permanent knee damage, then lying about it.

The lack of medical trust from country to country turned me into a bit of a medical expert myself. I packed extra equipment each trip in case the training situations continued to be less than ideal. Ankle braces, knee braces, tape, ice bags, forty-seven bottles of extra-strength ibuprofen replaced my Ed Hardy shirts. My suitcase no longer had room for all my stylish clothes, which was why, and the *only* reason why, I dressed so poorly back then.

These subtle differences, while not drastic, took a mental toll each season. Adjusting to a new time zone, language and culture was hard enough. Adding new referees, new rules and new responsibilities on top of the pressures of professional basketball made the first few weeks a living hell. The experience was unlike any job I've encountered. Most of the time, you know what you are getting into before accepting the position. With overseas professional basketball, I knew very little before I arrived and even less after. While stressful, this allowed me to embrace change better.

In the end, I was able to take away a few valuable lessons, like adapting to situations outside my control, something I had previously struggled with. I still cringe anytime I hear a whistle. That sound brings me back to those stressful situations; having to walk a fine line between aggressive and timid. It has, however, taught me a valuable lesson about my treatment of referees. How as a parent, I need to show more restraint than I did as a player. Because after all, I was once that young referee, just trying to buy beer and maybe get laid.

Chapter 13

Mentality

I had a routine. It never wavered. I would go hard in pregame warmups, generating enough sweat to create a decent-sized puddle on the floor underneath my locker. I would pop off my shooting shirt, wipe the perspiration from the surface of my skin, then lay my jersey on my knee and study the name, the number, the logo and the sponsors. Studying this piece of fabric put all my frustrations with overseas basketball into some sort of perspective. The crippling loneliness, as all my loved ones were back home. The aches and pains that encompassed every joint in my body. Staring at this memento made me realize it had all been worth it.

I'd then slip on my headphones and listen to the greatest hype song of all time, Busta Rhymes *Break Ya Neck*. During those three minutes and fifty-two seconds of intense psyching up, I would put my jersey on, lay on the ground, and stretch out my back and knees while nodding my head to the insane beat. Our coach would come in, I'd push pause, then listen intently to the strategies he diagrammed on the board while visualizing myself in those specific scenarios. We would put our hands in, shout something in unison, and I would slip my headphones back on and listen to the words that would mentally put me into the correct frame of mind.

> *"It's amazing, I'm the reason*
> *Everybody fired up this evening*
> *I'm exhausted, barely breathing*
> *Holding on to what I believe in"*

Only twenty seconds of Kanye West's *Amazing* would play, but during those brief moments, my mind became right. I was ready to perform. Ready to go out and give my all in a game that occasionally scared the shit out of me. It's sad to say, but sometimes, I needed that extra motivation. I had to keep telling myself that I'm getting the chance to travel the world while playing basketball; this is something most kids dream of growing up. The dream of playing in an arena full of people crowded into the seats to see *ME*. I was the reason everyone was fired up that evening. It was a constant reminder to give my all every game, something I occasionally struggled with.

I was explaining this to a man at the local Wegmans, who, while passing me in the produce aisle, had inquired about my height, then my basketball career, and then more specifically, if I had any routines. I spoke to him about the many superstitions I had, things like high socks and pregame meals, and how they varied in different situations. He seemed very impressed.

"You were able to travel the world playing basketball," he said, shaking his head in disbelief. "What an incredible opportunity!"

And he was right. It was an incredible opportunity. But while the chance of playing overseas was a rare mix of luck, hard work and genetic lottery, the mental struggles were definitely hard to overcome. I began telling him about the downside of playing overseas basketball. About the long trips and quick goodbyes. About the loneliness that sometimes becomes debilitating. I could see a confused look come across his face. The look that everyone gives when you badmouth a job they think is a dream. I was the insanely hot girl calling herself fat in front of her overweight friends.

"But you saw all of that just playing a game," he replied. I arched my head and pondered his comment.

It is how most people see basketball. They see the fame, the glitz, and the glam, but not the physical and mental toll it takes. Maintaining a proper mindset while playing overseas is very difficult. In fact, in some places, it is downright impossible. Some guys handle it well. For them being away from home is no big thing. After all, there are currently 108 international players competing in the NBA who don't seem too down but overseas is not the NBA.

I loved playing basketball abroad, but to honestly say I was never frustrated, depressed or lonely would be inaccurate. These are common feelings with the stresses involved in this profession; stresses like treating your body as a temple by performing constant sprints and counting your macros every day. Or sitting in an apartment completely alone, and in some cases bored out of your mind, to dealing with contractual issues in foreign countries, where nothing is guaranteed. Teams have the ability to cut you loose at any given time, giving the owner full control of your life. That is also the case with multi-year deals, a rarity in this world. Knowing that you are locked in for longer than a day would give the player some sense of normalcy and not the anxiety and panic of every few months figuring out where the next paycheck is coming from.

In overseas basketball, you have to deal with shady business practices and unethical human beings who have all the power while you have none. There is no union to protect you. It is their word that is trusted. In some cases, to deal with injuries and, in some cases, third-world medical care could put your life in danger. There is a small window of opportunity to make money in this game, causing players to ignore risks and take jobs in war zones or other high-risk countries just to be in a better financial position. And finally, what I struggled with the most, having to be the best player on the floor every single time you play and the pressure that goes along with that.

Growing up, I never possessed the *Jordan Mentality*. All my friends loved Michael Jordan, showing up to dress-down days rocking his new shoes every year with their stupid jeans rolled and tucked. Meanwhile, I would show up with corduroys and LA Gear because buying new sneakers was not in the budget every six months. Along with the shoes, I also did not possess that killer instinct. Now don't get me wrong, I was competitive and always wanted to win, but I never looked at myself to be the one solely responsible for this. I knew I had to play a role, and my team would be successful. Being that I was not one of the rich snobby kids rocking the fresh J's and jumping onto every bandwagon, I leaned towards the guys who didn't score the points but did all the dirty work.

My intrigue was with a different Chicago Bull, Dennis Rodman. He had a certain approach to the game that was different than anyone else. He would score only five points but grab fifteen rebounds and lockdown anyone on defense. He encompassed what I wanted to be as a basketball player. Tough, blue-collar and a bit eccentric. He was the reason I wanted to dye my hair and get tattoos. I never related to the high scorers, which is probably why I never was much of a high scorer myself. As my career progressed and that part of my game was expected to progress as well, sometimes the pressure became overwhelming. When you play overseas, you are expected to be the man. They have enough role players. They bring you in to be Kobe. If you don't possess that mentality, it becomes difficult to fake.

Don't get it twisted; I could go out and drop thirty points on any given night. I spent hours and hours in the gym working on becoming a better scorer, but the pressure to do it consistently, game after game, created anxiety within me. And sometimes, that anxiety took over my mind and body.

Take the first-round playoff matchup during the 2006 Australian NBL season, for instance. My team, the Cairns Taipans, squared off against the South Dragons and future NBA star Joe Ingles. The crowd was louder than usual, but again, this game was more important than usual. The Taipans were hosting only their second playoff game in franchise history, and I was the young American import the fans were counting on to lead the team to victory. The town was buzzing the entire week leading up to the showdown. The Taipans were the only professional sports franchise representing the tropical resort city of Cairns and were held in high regard by the local community.

This was not my first rodeo. I had played in several big games before that day. I played in my high school Sectional Finals, the Collegiate Conference Championships, the NCAA Tournament and the D-League Playoffs, but always as the underdog. Therefore my mental approach to this game was, well, it was different. We were expected to win, and for some reason, that scared the shit out of me.

In prior games, like the 2001 NCAA Tournament matchup against one of the best college basketball teams ever assembled, there was a strong sense of *we are supposed to get our asses kicked, so go out there and have fun.* And that's how we played, with no fear or worry that would lead to regret. The final score, 95-52, showed the immovable confidence we displayed that night in Greensboro, North Carolina.

Pressure has a funny way of bringing out the best or the worst in oneself. That night in Cairns, I struggled to deal with the pressure. I had always been a decent free throw shooter, nothing spectacular, nothing terrible. I was the girl at the end of the bar that you glance at when you walk in, then after striking out all night with the hotties, suddenly looks better. Just average. I had not been terrific from the charity stripe as of late, and the Dragons knew that. Anytime I had a clear lane to the basket, I got fouled. They were going to make me earn everything from the line. And for seven shots, their plan was working.

Every other aspect of my game was on that night, as my final stat line of nineteen points and twelve rebounds proved. Scoring and rebounding were all instinctual. But on the free-throw line, the mental side of the game overtook the physical side. I can't really describe the feeling accurately. It was as if I was paralyzed by fear. My arms, which had shot hundreds of thousands of free throws, seized up.

After the first miss, I shook my arm, slightly confused. *Fucking relax, take a deep breath, and shoot the ball!* Clang! The ball bounced hard off the front of the rim. *Get it together!* Again, clang! The game would resume, and mentally I'd go back to being myself until I was fouled again. I'd walk back to the line telling myself over and over again that I could do it as my body slowly went catatonic.

Clang! Clang!! After each miss, the Cairns fans began throwing me some sort of pity party. The cheers grew louder and louder as I went through my pre-shot routine, as did the groans when I once again missed. I was completely embarrassed. That night I finished one for eight from the foul line only because I banked the last one in. My mind had created a fear so immense; it altered a routine I worked twenty years perfecting.

I still don't understand what happened. It was as if someone went back in time and stole my mojo. It took yoga, meditation, and lots of pressure-filled shots to try and regain control of my body on the free-throw line. I knew my brain was capable of incredible things. I never thought my brain could use that power for evil, to completely overtake my nervous system and undo years of progress.

I already had a problem with butterflies in my stomach before each game. It was a natural reaction to being nervous, a mentality that is easy to insult while watching games on your couch screaming at your television about how the athletes lack the proper mindset. But spoiler alert, athletes get nervous. Maybe not all athletes. I have played with a few remarkably confident guys who never once doubted themselves.

Mental toughness is not something born within each child. It is a trait that comes from the environment one grows up in. Kids who deal with more trauma growing up tend to have higher resilience to adverse situations. These situations allow the brain to process fear and doubt differently from someone who didn't have to process trauma at a young age. While more than some of my friends, my trauma was not on the high end of the psychological damage scale. My parents worked very hard to make sure we were never hungry, had a house to play in, and while the Philadelphia Eagles Starter Jacket that I coveted so much dangled out of our financial grasp, I grew up with a trauma-free existence.

I believe I never possessed the *Jordan Mentality* because I grew up wanting people to like me. I always tried my best to impress everyone and not be a social outcast, which did not always help my mindset walking on the court to play a game against my peers. If I sucked, they would laugh at me, which is why I did not love basketball as a kid. I love the game *now*. It is my life and gave me every opportunity I had. But I did not grow up with this mentality. I played because I was good, and I continued because I got better. I had the drive to improve and be the best, but the focus was not strictly on basketball. Being cool was more important than basketball, but because of my alien-like physique, playing basketball was the only way to be cool.

Little by little, I developed mental toughness on the basketball court. In high school, I sat the bench my freshman and sophomore years, which had more to do with a late growth spurt that jumped me from a 6-foot 2-inch one-hundred-fifty-pound fifteen-year-old to a 6-foot 10-inch one-hundred-ninety pound teenager in a little over a year. This sizable stretch increased my ever-growing lack of coordination. By senior year, I had learned to move with all my extra parts despite being remarkably skinny. Occasionally a football player was deployed to *neutralize* my height, and I had to adjust. A frightening experience, as people with big muscles scared me. Mainly because I had none and they had lots. This was not helped by my coach's constant yelling at me to "go through the contact" when all I wanted to do was avoid it. While I was not scared of scrapping for a rebound, diving on a loose ball, or taking a charge, I wasn't big on confrontations with strong dudes. I'd taken my share of shots from them in the past and never stood up for myself. Even as my muscles grew, I still was not comfortable in physical confrontations. Then in stepped Randall Orr.

I do not know why I remembered his name. People tell me their names all the time, and most of the time, I forget it before releasing the grip of the handshake. But Randall "Randy" Orr always stuck with me. Maybe because he was my first nemesis and the turning point from the hard-working sort of bitch to potential tough guy, badass.

Because of my need to please, I do not believe anyone ever hated me. My college roommate and close friend, Jay Law, once told me he hated me during our freshman year because, according to him, I was tall and annoying and cocky, and the girls all laughed at my jokes. But Jay and I since became close friends to this day, and the hate was short-lived. But I am pretty sure, at that time and possibly now, Randall Orr fucking hated me.

He played for several NBA D-League teams over two years, and we seemed to play against each other an awful lot. The D-League only had six teams; therefore, playing the same team four times in a row was not that uncommon. It so happened that Randall would play for the team we repeatedly played, then be traded to the team we were scheduled to play repeatedly. This set the stage for some aggressive matchups as we both played the same position, and the D-League was not gentle.

My toughness slowly progressed. Teammates in college described me as The Incredible Hulk, and not for the cool reasons. More like, I was a bitch until I got mad, and then I was unstoppable. Growing up, I had a decent amount of patience. It would take a significant amount of adversity to get me mad, which is what my fellow teammates noticed. I was pretty chill. Not really aggressive or antagonistic, but more levelheaded, that was until I reached my fill. When I got pissed, I got really pissed. At that point, I would reach crazy levels of anger, and my mind would go into a different place. It is why there are still posters covering up the many holes in my mom's attic. Those were from me losing my patience.

These hulk-outs were beneficial for our team's success on the court, but as I mentioned previously, it would take a good amount of adversity to get me there. I played with several players who had a winner's mentality. They would make me hulk-out all the time in practice but found it difficult to do so in the game, seeing as we were fighting a common enemy and I was not going to get pissed at them when I already had to be pissed at the other team. Playing with me during that time was undoubtedly frustrating, as they saw how aggressive I could be when angry but getting that aggressiveness to come out was unpredictable.

Randall Orr was the first person that helped me harness my unique abilities, unbeknownst to him. In fact, I am certain Orr doesn't even remember me. To him, I was just some asshole who pissed him off, but for me, he was the turning point.

We had already played the Huntsville Flight eight times during the 2004-2005 season. Randall and I had matched up against each other during those battles. There was an elbow here or there. I think he had a hard dunk and called me a pussy but nothing along the Bill Laimbeer-Charles Barkley level. Being that it was 2005 and I was not checking the transactions for other teams, I thought it was odd to see him warming up two weeks later for our first of four games against the Columbus Riverdragons, the team who had recently acquired him.

There is another thing I should mention. When I was not in Hulk mode, I tended to avoid confrontation. I was not talking trash or instigating altercations. I was just playing basketball. I did not realize how important having that dark side would be. Therefore, after the first two games in Roanoke, I had taken some physical and verbal abuse. I had played well and, like I saw Tim Duncan do numerous times before, stayed focused and did not engage in anything extracurricular. That was not reciprocated. The River Dragon front court let me know every time something went their way. There was some name-calling, a shove after the whistle blew, and during a scramble for a loose ball, my head was pinned against the hardwood by Orr's forearm. I remember getting up and seeing him laugh. "What are you gonna do?" he shouted. The final buzzer sounded just a few seconds later, and we headed off to shower, pack and get on the bus for a nine-hour drive to Columbus, Georgia.

During that long, dark ride, I thought about what was said to me, how I was being perceived as a pushover. The rage began growing, but this time it was not going away. The following evening Orr and I squared off for the tenth time that season. This time the rage still burned. I was always taught to be levelheaded, that brains will always beat brawn. That night I said fuck all that. This was personal.

I was a complete dickhead from the opening tip. I ran down the court and slammed into Orr for a post seal which sent him tumbling to the floor. I turned and dunked the ball before staring him down and asking, "Who's the pussy now?"

"Oh, ok. It's like that?" he replied.

The back and forth went on for three quarters. Twice we were tangled up, and some shoving ensued, the last of which got us double technical fouls. My coach was not happy with my terrible attitude and sat me down. That just pissed me off more. With just minutes left in a close game, I re-entered at the same time as my nemesis. His team held a slight lead at that point, and every mistake became monumental.

My Dazzle BFF, Seth Doliboa, held the ball out front as we set up for a shot. Our best shooter, Sung Yoon Bang, shot across the lane right off my screen. The call of *switch* went out, and Orr, who was playing off me at the time, became responsible for guarding Bang. Orr took three hard steps and tried to run me over in order to get through my screen. I noticed his bull rush and shifted my weight. He came full force at me, and I used his momentum to body slam him into the hardwood like Hulk Hogan on Andre the Giant. He did not appreciate this distasteful move, and we tussled on the floor some more.

I popped up quickly and stood over him while he still laid facing the ground. As he got to his knees, I noticed his hand had balled into a fist. He was going to fight me. This was it, fight or flight time. The old me would have walked away, avoiding any confrontation, but the new me stood over him and whispered, "I wish you would." Orr became irate and hopped to his feet, ready to throw down, before being restrained by his teammates. I stood unwavering, staring at him with zero fear.

This was unprecedented. I had always walked away from fights, but not this time. I was patient and calm, but at the same time, completely enraged. My inner Hulk was finally ready. I did not back away or move. Instead, I wished he would punch me in the face so I could unload on him like Ralphie from a *Christmas Story* after he had enough of Scott Farkus' shit. To any normal basketball player, this was a normal occurrence., something that happened every game. I was never a blip on Randall Orr's radar, just a random opponent on a random night. But for me, this was my do-or-die moment. I was able to eventually channel that rage into being a productive basketball player.

Heading into a game without the fear that someone was going to beat me up made focusing on basketball that much easier. Even if it occasionally came and went, I had an easier time controlling the rage that would build up inside of me. I would be able to channel it into something productive while creating ways for my brain to overcome obstacles and be tough in the face of adversity. Most of the stories I laughed off just because of the sheer lunacy of them. The stories I couldn't laugh off were not as grandiose. They were the bouts of sadness and depression that sometimes became debilitating.

Many factors contributed to my depression, like the mental grind of never being my own boss and having someone telling me what to do my whole life. Answering the media and fans every time something went wrong. Missing weddings, bachelor parties, and other fun activities because I spent most of my 20s, a time when most people are out making bad decisions, forced to be an adult far away from home. I never wanted to feel left out. I never wanted to feel alone. But for eight years, I was just that, isolated from my family and friends. That loneliness took a toll. There is nothing worse than coming home after a bad game to an empty apartment in a faraway place, with no one to talk to and no one to help you through it.

This loneliness reached its nexus when I was in Kosovo. The combination of anxiety, lack of confidence, and complete mental exhaustion turned the game I loved into a game I hated. My anger was getting the best of me, and I wanted to quit. I was done with basketball. I was far from home, completely isolated from the world. My knee hurt, my back hurt and medical attention was non-existent. My only communication with the outside world was through Skype and AOL Instant Messenger.

Then after a tough game where I fouled out and twisted my knee while on a Skype call home, my power went out. I sat in the dark and finally broke. I began crying, alone in the pitch black. Growing up, I never cried much. Crying was a weakness, and I was a big boy. But the tears were not stopping. I had emotionally snapped, and the dark Kosovo night was not helping. I went into my now warm refrigerator, where I had eight beers leftover from a previous night out. I was never a big drinker, despite what the five guys who carried me to the subway at my bachelor party said. But there I was, drinking to numb the pain. Every time the depression crawled back, I downed another beer. This went on for several hours until I eventually passed out.

I never have before nor after being in such a dark mental place. There were many times I told myself I was going to quit playing. I was going to march into practice and tell them to book me a flight home. But to quit after waiting seven months to play was not a possibility. I had worked too hard to get here, but my mind was breaking down. I didn't have Melatonin or any other sleep aid, so alcohol became my tranquilizer. It was the only way I could fall asleep. So, I drank my way through the season. My depressed state did not stop when I went home. I still drank too much, trying to forget that I was now the kid no one wanted. It took a promising writing career and some help from loved ones to pull me out of that funk. My drinking slowed, and my exercising increased. Eventually, I was back to myself and the positive outlook on life I always possessed.

I still don't know why I decided to play another year. I was already mentally checked out, but my ego got in the way. I knew no other life besides being a basketball player. All my friends had normal jobs. I stood out. I was successful and did not want to relinquish that title. So, I told my agent to keep looking for jobs. When I finally retired, it was a sense of relief. Looking back now, as most people do when they gain wisdom with age, I would love to still be playing. To be exploring the world and meeting new people. But that was not where my mind was back then. I looked at the finality as an end to eight hours per day workouts or leaving home within a day's notice to be alone in a foreign country, filled with people who expected me to be the savior for their specific team.

"You're right," I said to the gentleman in Wegmans as I tilted my head back and tossed the plastic bag filled with spinach into my Wegmans cart. "It is just a game. And I did appreciate my career. But if you understand one thing, it is that to you, basketball is a game. To me, it was a job. I bet the Oompa Loompas were pissed when they had to extract Augustus Gloop from the Fudge Room. Every job has its upsides, and every job has its downfalls. The shittier the situation, the shittier the mentality becomes. That's just life, I guess."

The man nodded and adjusted his glasses. "You certainly have a different perspective than other athletes I have heard."

"Maybe," I said. "Or maybe the other athletes just told you what you wanted to hear."

Chapter 14

Symbolism

I spent the night before my ninth birthday watching *The Lost Boys*, another R-rated gem that probably contributed to some of the psychological damage I suffer from today. My sister Paulette and every other American female teenager in the '80s were obsessed with Corey Haim. Being that I was not a love-struck teenage girl, I gravitated more towards the Frog Brothers, the Ramboesque teenage assassins hellbent on saving Santa Monica from a vampire overtaking. Shortly after the constant nightmares ceased, I began wearing the navy-blue plaid ties which accompanied my Catholic grade school uniform as a headband. I'd chase my ten-year-old Irish Wolfhound around the house with a mini baseball bat imagining it was a stake and she, a blood-thirsty teenage vampire. The tie, although intimidating and great for keeping the long bangs my mom refused to cut out of my eyes, was not badass enough. I knew if Kiefer Sutherland showed up at my door, my school tie and the wooden bat would not be enough to save my family from certain doom.

This look was missing a certain something. Something that screamed, "NOT TODAY BLOODSUCKER!" I rifled through my dad's junk drawer and pulled out a black permanent marker. I walked to the mirror. On my left shoulder, I began drawing a very crude rendering of the skull and crossbones from the pirate hat I wore the previous Halloween. The entire time trying to avoid passing out from the fumes emitted from the toxic chemicals, which made the markers permanent.

The outfit was now complete! Not a single vampire would fuck with me now, not with my headband, not with my stake, and definitely not with this tattoo. I envisioned encountering those lost boys on a dark boardwalk. They would fly down teeth bared, see me with my blue plaid tie with the yellow lines wrapped tightly around my head, my sharpened Von Hayes autographed mini-bat and my badass skull and crossbones tattoo. They'd look at each other in horror and fly away to another county, far away from my jurisdiction.

I spent that day running through my backyard, working on my barrel rolls, and stabbing the beat-up punching bag which hung behind the shed. After a few hours of perfecting my form, my dad returned from work and walked back to see what my overactive imagination had gotten me into that day. One look at his face, and I knew I had done something he was not pleased with. I felt I was going to get one of the lectures I had heard so many times before, where he sat me down and sternly taught me the difference between doing the right thing and doing the wrong thing. But this was different. The fire in his eyes burned bright enough for me to know that this was not going to be a lecture on vampires not being real or why I should not have sharpened the Von Hayes bat.

He glared at my arm, then back in my eyes, and yelled, "KEVIN, IF YOU EVER GET A TATTOO, I'M GOING TO TAKE IT OFF WITH A CHEESE GRATER!"

Little did I know that quote would run through my head many years later as I walked into the red sterilized room filled with paintings of warriors and goddesses. The art was painted by the man who would soon be using my skin as his new easel, my tattoo artist Matt Doherty.

I would like to say I heeded my father's warning before that moment and never again permanently marked up my skin, but it would not be true. As a sophomore at Monmouth University after our miraculous bid to the NCAA Tournament, we celebrated like young, stupid, early twenty-somethings celebrate milestones. We went back to a campus that was on spring recess and drank Keystone Light in an empty apartment with a stereo system, a pack of CDs and a handful of cheerleaders who did not leave for Cancun immediately following the final buzzer. Being that it was a male-dominated, testosterone-fueled party and the fact that all the cheerleaders were trying to have sex with our Jim Morrison look-alike forward, Jay Dooley, we began declaring ourselves brothers forever. This deal was to be sealed with matching tattoos, etching the victory into our skin for all of eternity.

When I sobered up the following evening (it was a hell of a party), I went to the dining hall and met up with my comrades. Cameron Milton, our tough-as-nails guard from Philadelphia, looked up at me and asked, "Kev, you thought about what tattoo you're getting?"

Oh shit! I realized the empty promise I made while standing on a couch shit-faced the night before was actually going to happen. I had to get a tattoo. There was no way around it. I could not betray my team and bail out on our promise, especially after recalling that this was my drunken idea.

Sweat beaded down my neck as I sat in the back of Cam's car while we drove through the cold West Long Branch night a few weeks later. Upon much deliberation, I had decided that I wanted a Superman logo surrounded by some sort of tribal design. This was the early 2000s, and the word tribal meant thick, black lines with sharp edges and absolutely no association to any tribe or culture in the world. Also, Superman because I was a dork growing up and would spend rainy days inside reading comic books imaging, I was a hero to someone. Getting a tattoo was more important than the actual tattoo design itself. Therefore when you walk along the beach these days, you see mothers carrying children around with an awful reminder of their sexual escapades at Senor Frogs, Cancun circa 1998, on their lower back.

We spent a few minutes paging through the assortment of designs that hung on the walls. There was a dragon, Chinese symbols, and for some reason, an absurd number of naked women. I assume those naked women were for whatever perv couldn't get a woman to take her clothes off and needed to be permanently reminded of that image.

My teammates settled on designs in the display, as for many, this was not their first tattoo. They were brought into different rooms while I discussed my idea with what you imagine the stereotypical image of a tattoo artist would be. He was bearded with a bandanna and leather vest, with an assortment of tattoos up and down his arms. "Where?" he muttered without looking up from the fog of the cigarette hanging from his lips.

This is where things took a weird turn. I was twenty years old at the time but still feared my father. He was an extremely tall, strong, stern and prone to angry outbursts. I knew I had to keep up with the solidarity of my teammates but knew I did not want a cheese grater scar on my arm for eternity.

"Um..I...think...um...my right thigh," I told him. He stopped what he was doing and slowly looked up at me, the cigarette still hanging from his lips.

"Your right thigh?" he repeated back to me.

"Yes, sir," I replied nervously.

He went back down to his drawing, erased it and restarted. "OK," he said, a little confused with a whole lot judgment. I had found the ultimate compromise, I would share in the tattoo experience with my team and hide the logo from my parents, who I envisioned would never see me in a speedo. It was a perfect crime!

Well, almost perfect. When my teammates found out the location, they told me that it was a spot reserved for females. And almost perfect because I forgot to wear my long spandex for a game the following season, leaving my tattooed thigh susceptible to exposure under my shorts. And that susceptible tattooed thigh became exposed a few minutes into the first half of a game while I wrestled for a loose ball. My legs elevated into the air, my shorts bunched up towards my junk, and a large black mix of symbolism and thick, sharp, black lines on display for the world, including my mom, to see. After the game, my mother, worried that I had developed the onset of the Black Plague, asked what was residing on my leg. I explained myself as she shook her head in disappointment. We never spoke of it again.

The memories of that initial tattoo rushed through my mind while I sat in a plush black chair waiting for Matt to begin my next inscribing. This tattoo would not be hidden by shorts, pants or tie bandanas and would leave me vulnerable to cheese grater attacks. Fourteen years and 201,493 miles between trips to the tattoo parlor had given me a wider knowledge of the world and the reasoning and origin of tattoos.

Allen Iverson introduced tattoos into my world when he donned a Sixers jersey and began his Hall of Fame career. He would later knock over my Gatorade in frustration when we worked out together under the tutelage of John Hardnett and Fred Douglas in Philadelphia. I didn't say a word to him, nor did he apologize, but it was one of the more memorable moments I ever had on the sidelines of a basketball court. Tattoos, I would discover when I left the United States, had been around for thousands of years. Culturally, tattoos were symbolic and considered a visual representation of one's accomplishments. Here in America, the thought process for tattoos was far less symbolic. I am not sure what barbed wire wrapping around one's bicep signifies, but it definitely isn't a badge of honor.

New Zealand was my first experience dealing with people who held prominent jobs and had tattoos. It was culturally new and unexpected. It also opened my eyes to how people with tattoos should be perceived. Not as a criminal or vampire hunter, but as someone who wants to visually portray their achievements. It was around that time when I began designing the tattoo I would have engraved in my skin when I retired. It would contain a representation of each culture I immersed myself in throughout my basketball career.

It started with a globe attached to a large wing to represent the Hawks of Monmouth University, a Maori storyline for my time in New Zealand, and the six stars of Kosovo representing the six different ethnic groups. Also, the Korean word for perseverance, an attribute I needed a fuckload of in South Korea. The phrase World Traveler, written in Estonian as MAAILMA REISIJA, above the Roman Numeral XV (15), my number throughout most of my professional career. The stars of the Southern Cross Constellation, which adorn the Australian flag. And finally, eight different stars for the eight different uniforms I wore, the largest representing the Roanoke Dazzle and the large star that illuminated the city each night high above Mill Mountain. These designs would artistically be tied together with the coordinates of each location.

As Matt's tattoo gun began buzzing, I had a flashback of the pain endured during my Superman logo creation. He looked me in the eye and asked, "You ready?"

I nodded, took a deep breath and replied, "Yep." The buzzing grew louder and louder until it connected with my skin causing my muscles to tense up. I began to think if the stinky marker from twenty-five years ago would have been a better option. The first flesh-piercing needle brought with it pain and also a strange calm.

The anxiety I felt about the permanence of this new arm art suddenly washed away. I was confident in my decision. The tattoo was going to be a constant reminder of both the good times and the bad times. The song *You're Welcome* from the Disney movie Moana kept replaying in my mind. Probably because my daughter and I watched it over one hundred times before this experience. Specific verses of Maui's words resonated with me, most notably:

> *"And the tapestry here on my skin*
> *Is a map of the victories I win*

Look where I've been
I make everything happen
Look at that mini-Maui just tippity-tappin'"'

It took all of my power not to start dancing to the beat of Dwayne Johnson's catchy tune for fear that I would leave a permanent unintentional typo on my arm. These words, while from a children's movie, held significance to me. My tattoo would be a map of the victories I won. Not just physical victories on the basketball court, but victories over self-doubt, anxiety and fear, the three things I struggled with throughout my life. And sometimes, these victories were not victories in the literal sense of the word. Sometimes the battle was not always a total win. I thought back to my time in South Korea, pushing my body to its natural limits, even when my joints were begging me to stop. When my knee refused to take any more abuse and snapped, I still kept going. Or in Kosovo, when I sat alone in the dark suffering from insomnia and depression, wishing, crying for home, I refused to be an example of regret. I already had enough regret in my life.

From a young age, it was drilled into my head to never have any regrets. To make sure I played every game like it was my last. No matter how hard I tried, I still have regret. Regret that I was never able to sub into a game and hear the announcer call out, "Now checking in for the Philadelphia 76ers, number fifteen, Kevin Owens."

I didn't care what number. I didn't care what team. I just wanted the feeling I saw many players achieve throughout my career. Never fully making it in the NBA has been a mental struggle for me every day since I hung up my jersey. *What if I worked a little harder? What if I concentrated a little more?* Playing professional basketball was the hardest thing I've ever done. It took a mental and physical toll on my body. I worked extremely hard but came up short. And that is something I have to deal with for the rest of my life. Being so close, but never really knowing.

It was like my Sophomore Cotillion date with Becky. How do I know what could have been? Was I ever even close, or did I never have a shot? Maybe a team somewhere looked at me and thought, *we should sign this guy*, but then an act of God occurred, and it never materialized. Or maybe like Becky, I was never close at all.

I frequently go back to my first night of that initial exposure camp, where I laid under the stars wondering how I could face the orgy participants the following day and the mortification that would follow. It makes me realize how far I have come from the skinny, shy, scared kid hiding in the bed of my truck to the strong, confident man who would have told everyone to take the party elsewhere because I needed to sleep. However, while my confidence has grown, that hint of regret still dances in the back of my mind. That phrase repeated over and over, *Were you good enough?*

This philosophical debate resonated in my brain while the steel needle delivering ink into the dermis of my skin created a cold, burning sensation. I reminisced on the memories of my basketball career and how I would be remembered by the countless people who saw me play. More importantly, how will I be remembered by my daughter, who hopefully, after reading this when she is older, will realize that her dad was not just a normal dad, but a cool dad.

Will I be remembered as the guy standing behind a barrier of plastic while an onslaught of metal, glass and flares was lethally thrown at my head? Or maybe I'll be the guy with high socks who couldn't make a free throw but rebounded the shit out of the ball. Or the guy that finally stood up to a bully after spending his whole life being a punching bag. Would I be the skinny kid with zero confidence who, for a second, thought he could successfully navigate the pitfalls of adolescence and finally get the girl? Or the hard-nosed, tough guy who never quit and never stopped fighting. Maybe I'll be remembered as the guy with long hair who, for some reason, had his shirt off at the bar a lot. Or the guy wandering through the snow in a pair of flip-flops. Or maybe, just maybe, I could be all of these.

Maybe my experiences could be a memory for someone else, like the young fan holding my jersey on the sideline of a random Estonian arena. Maybe my effort created his drive. Maybe I became his Dennis Rodman. Maybe his dream was just to play one game under the bright lights of Estonia. Maybe when he walks off the court for the final time, he will give his jersey to a fan and realize he made it. He achieved his dream. And maybe, just maybe, I can look back on my career, the many successes and the many failures, the laughter, the tears, the pain of injuries, or just the pain of a hangover. Maybe when I glance down at the tattoo adorning my arm, I can realize I achieved mine too.

Epilogue

Anytime my friends would come over, my stepdad thought he'd be funny. I could always count on him proclaiming to everyone, "You can pick your friends, you can pick your nose, but you can't pick your friend's nose."

He would laugh and continue with what he was doing. I never thought twice about it until that phrase began passing through my head anytime I reflected on my friendships.

I have always held my friends in high regard. Growing up I was around my brothers and sister a good amount of time. But my sister was much older and eventually went away to college, then Geoff, my stepbrother and I were left to our own devices. My friends filled that void. They became family. I have known them all since I was an incredibly awkward skinny kid. They had just as much of a role as anyone in shaping who I am and what I have become. Each of them had high goals, and each of them chased and achieved their dreams. They are truly a great group of guys who care deeply about me, which they will never admit to, and immediately text our group chat stating that they don't, if they ever read this book, which they probably won't.

So, let me start again. My friends are dicks.

I always judge a solid friendship based on distance. Being that distance and friendships have gone hand in hand in my life, I have gained some experience in the matter. The best way to truly define a friendship is by having that distance, then after a few months or even years apart, nothing changes. Same conversations, same comfort, same laughter—just picking up right where you left off.

I've had many solid friendships over the years. Many came from the players I shared the court with. I still talk to my high school teammates, my college teammates, and even though I have not seen many of them in over a decade, my professional teammates. We text and Facetime from time to time, but besides the time I went up to NYC to hang out with my former rebounding mate in New Zealand, Nick Horvath, a virtual friendship is all we have had.

This is why when Seth Doliboa, my NBA G-League colleague, called me out of the blue on a Tuesday night ten years after I retired from professional basketball, I immediately picked up. Seth, his wife and son, were traveling home from a tropical vacation and had missed a connecting flight and subsequently had to stay in a hotel next to the Philadelphia Airport. Because we played two full seasons together, I look at Seth as a close friend even though we had not seen each other in twelve years.

I drove twenty minutes from my home in Cherry Hill, a suburb of Philadelphia, to the airport hotel for an impromptu rendezvous. It was a few days before Christmas, and I had just bought a fantastic Santa Claus tee from Old Navy that I felt needed to be worn on that seventeen-degree winter evening sans jacket. I briskly walked through the cold parking lot to meet up with my old friend.

I was greeted in the lobby by my 6-foot 8-inch former teammate. "Why the fuck are you wearing a t-shirt?" he asked. I smiled, shrugged my shoulders and we bro hugged. "Haven't changed a bit," Seth said with a smile.

The conversation picked up right where we left off, laughing at inside jokes about our teammates' sexual experiences and laughing about how Seth used to constantly mess with our 7-foot 3-inch center, Peter Ramos, calling him Peterman. We picked up right where we left off. It was like we never left.

We sat down on a couch in the festively decorated hotel lobby bar. I had been intermittently fasting for the past year, trying to avoid becoming an unathletic-looking former athlete. So when Seth brought me over a beer around nine o'clock at night, there was a slight panic as drinking anything besides water between the hours of eight at night to noon the next day could set off a chain reaction of fat storage in my body, that for some reason, settles directly into my sides.

"I got you a Stella," he said as he handed me the bottle. "I know you always liked drinking weird fancy beers."

"Thanks," I laughed. "So full disclosure, I have been doing this fasting thing for like a year, so I won't become a fat person. This is the first time I have drank a beer after eight o' clock at night in months."

Seth raised his eyebrow and gave me a judgmental side-eye. "Umm, ok," he replied, smirking. "I guess I can drink it."

"No, it's cool," I told him, shaking off the embarrassment that I had become some sort of d-bag adult who refuses a beer from a close friend I had not seen in years because of side fat.

Since we were both entering the fourth decade of our lives, the conversations dealt mainly with adulting-type things. Parenting, bad knees, what sort of vitamins we take. Shit like that. Occasionally a story from the past would come up, and we would laugh and reminisce.

"Talk to me about your business," I stated, finally deciding it was time to get down to the real shit.

"Yeah, so I co-own a custom home developing company, building houses and developments with my brother," Seth replied. "It's stressful at times with the market, but when things are good, they are good." Seth had briefly retired from professional basketball after our time together in the D-League and worked for his dad building houses. Once the housing market crashed in 2007, he went back through the exposure camp gauntlet and restarted his professional basketball career. He ended up playing seven more seasons, mainly in Portugal, before heading home and finally taking over the family company Catalyst Custom Homes.

"What about you?" he asked.

Oh shit! I dreaded this part of the conversation. Not that I didn't love what I did, it just wasn't the money-making post-basketball career I had dreamed of. "Well," I replied. "I'm teaching and coaching basketball." Seth nodded his head and took a drink from his beer. "I am also writing a book about my playing career," I blurted out.

"Wow, that is awesome! Am I in the book?"

"Yeah. You are a featured story."

"That's really cool."

"Thanks. The process is hard as shit, but hopefully, it turns into something good." I crossed my fingers.

"So do you like teaching."

Damn, I thought we were done talking about me. Yeah. Sure. It's great. Dealing with hormone-raged young adults is exactly what I thought I would be doing after retirement. No amount of defensive drills during basketball practice can teach you how to deal with the parents of the children you're supposed to be guiding through life. No amount of offensive drills can prepare you for the drama after a classroom breakup occurs. "Yeah. Sure," I replied, "It's great."

While my job was rewarding in terms of how many human beings I have bettered and helped, it did not provide the monetary gains I was accustomed to when I held a different title. I tried multiple times to steer the conversation back to multi-vitamins but was unsuccessful. Seth owned a very successful business after basketball retirement, and life was treating him well. I, on the other hand, was a teacher making little money and getting even less respect. Not that I was jealous of Seth. I was very proud. It was just knowing where I was and what I have become was a little frustrating. I thought back to the phrase untapped potential. I had to do something to get me back on the map, back to the fame and fortune that led me to be a professional athlete in the first place.

That night driving home after two beers that immediately built up in my back fat pockets and a few hours of storytelling and laughing with my good friend, I thought about our conversation. How did I get here? How did I transition from pro sports to a job? What connections did I use? Who helped me? And who did not return my calls? How hard was it to get hired after playing in foreign countries for ten years and having zero experience?

It hit me like a shot to the balls. I know what happened to me when I was no longer overseas famous, but what about everyone else? Do they miss the bright lights? Has anyone else gone into teaching? Did anyone ever collect the money that was rightfully theirs? I wanted to hear other's stories; the good, the bad, the ugly, and the crazy.

I became motivated. It was time to become once again overseas famous. These men and women who held such illustrious positions in professional sports had a story to tell, and I was prepared to listen.

When I arrived home, I looked through my phone and noticed one number that intrigued me. "What's up" I sent a text message out to a former player who was just starting his overseas career as I was ending mine. My phone buzzed a minute later.

"Yo, KO! Just got back from Germany a few weeks ago."

"Nice," I replied. "You know what you are doing next year?"

"Not this," he texted back. "I'm hanging them up."

"Really? So, what's your plan?"

"KO, I have no fucking clue! To tell you the truth, I have sat through so many orientations talking about the future and plans for retirement, and to be honest, all I ever thought about was hooping. Someone should write a book with a blueprint for how to transition from being a pro athlete."

"I'm on it!"

About the Author

Kevin Owens is a veteran of overseas professional basketball and a current teacher and basketball coach. He is an entrepreneur and founder of Overseas Famous LLC, a multimedia platform created to give athletes playing abroad a voice. These stories provide a behind-the-scenes look at what goes on with overseas sports. He's a fitness enthusiast who has dabbled in triathlons despite having only a small percentage of one arthritic knee left. Most importantly, he is the father to his amazing daughter Olivia. He lives in Cherry Hill, NJ, and is a rabid Philadelphia sports fan. While he had the name first, he is now the second most popular Kevin Owens in the world.

Made in the USA
Middletown, DE
17 August 2021